The
Red Hills
of Home

The RED HILLS of HOME

S.L. CLAYTOR & J.W. SEARS

Darter Lane Books

Darter Lane
Books

Copyright © 2020 by S.L. Claytor

All rights reserved.

No part of this publication may be reproduced in whole or in part, distributed, scanned, uploaded, stored in a database or retrieval system, or transmitted in any form or by any means, including electronic or mechanical, photocopy, recording, or otherwise, without the prior written permission of the author (except in the case of brief quotations embodied in critical articles and reviews).

This is a work of creative nonfiction, written by S.L. Claytor from stories told by Georgia Boy Red. The events are portrayed to the best of Georgia Boy Red's memory, and he has done his best to recreate events, locales, and conversations from his memories. This work reflects his present recollections of his earlier life experiences and coming of age, but it is hard to remember every detail after so many years, and in instances where facts could not be remembered or verified, the author has filled in those gaps with reimagined scenes that she believes maintains the essence of the events as experienced by Georgia Boy Red. While the stories in this book are true, some minor embellishments have been added for literary purposes, some names and identifying details have been changed to protect the privacy of the people involved, some events have been compressed, and some dialogue has been recreated.

ISBN-13: 978-1-950900-06-0
ISBN-10: 1-950900-06-1

DEDICATIONS

J.W. Sears (Georgia Boy Red) dedicates this book to
his wife, his three daughters, and to all of his
friends and family mentioned within these
pages who have had the privilege to
call Handtown home.

S.L. Claytor dedicates this book to
the man who lived these stories—
Georgia Boy Red.

Remembrances of the past. The good ol' days. I will always cherish these fond memories that shaped who I am. Thinking back, I laugh, and I cry, for a part of my heart will forever lie in the red hills of home.

Georgia Boy Red

CONTENTS

Preface	Pg xiii
Prologue	Pg 3
A Simpler Place & Time	Pg 7
The Early Years	Pg 22
All Forgiven	Pg 36
Bad Experiences	Pg 50
Waycross Woes	Pg 62
Early Teen Years	Pg 76
Thankful for Daddy	Pg 89
Bad Choices	Pg 101
Tobacco Crops & Turpentine Trees	Pg 111
Handtown Haunts	Pg 120
Latter Teen Years	Pg 132
Drafted	Pg 145
In the Army Now	Pg 158
Epilogue	Pg 177

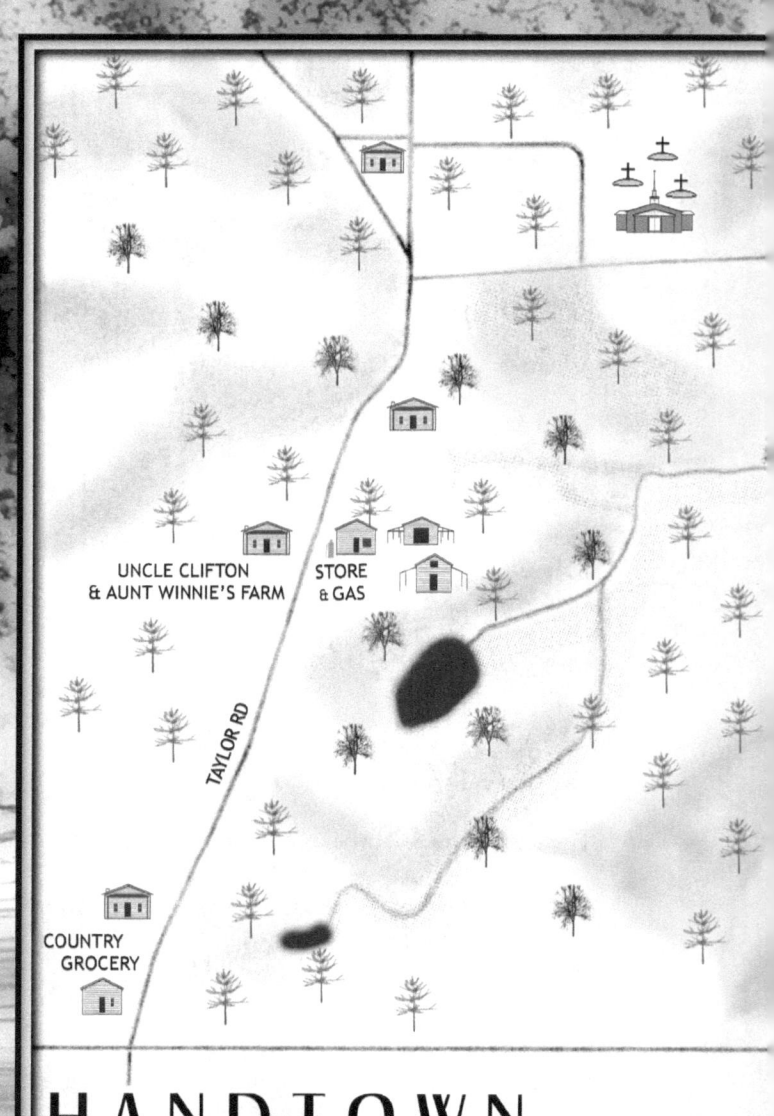

HANDTOWN

PREFACE

I began this project for the purpose of preserving a loved one's childhood stories of a bygone time. When I started writing Georgia Boy Red's coming-of-age biography, being a collaborative work between author and storyteller, I initially chose a third-person point of view; however, after completing the first chapter, I felt something was lacking. It became abundantly clear to me that although the subject was not the author, the perspective needed to be changed to a first-person point of view—I would be his voice—a perspective that captured a personal connection not achieved in my first draft—a sense of nostalgia that I, myself, experienced while sitting and listening to Georgia Boy Red tell of his humble beginnings and carefree childhood days while growing up in the southernmost hills of Georgia from the early 1930s to the 1950s.

    I refer to this book as creative nonfiction. Even though it is written as a memoir, and the stories are true,

I have embroidered instances where facts could not be remembered or verified. I have filled in gaps, recreated dialogue, and have included information obtained through research relating to that time long past. I have given every effort to maintain the true essence in each of Georgia Boy Red's stories; however, there is no expectation of complete accuracy of dates and dialogue from so long ago, as time robs memories of precious details. Let me reiterate what is stated in the book's disclaimer, that the events are portrayed to the best of Georgia Boy Red's memory.

I would like to acknowledge two people who lent a bit of information during the writing of this work—Ronald and Shirley. I know those red hills of home hold the same high degree of meaning to you as they do to your big brother, Georgia Boy Red.

S.L. Claytor, January 3, 2020

The RED HILLS of HOME

PROLOGUE

October 2020

Handtown Community, Hazlehurst, Ga

Timber, stacked to the rafters, filled the remnants of an old crib barn nestled amid several aged oak trees on land that was once my homestead. The ramshackle outbuilding with its rusting tin, collapsed lean-to shed roof sides, and missing door looked lonesome...forgotten.

    I stood in the middle of Yawn Cemetery Road, a red clay byway that traveled across the hills where I grew up, and I stared at the skeletal barn, remembering how it looked long ago. My gaze then traveled to where our little farmhouse once stood, situated close to the road, beyond an old chinaberry tree that in days long past had shaded our front yard but now looked tired and frail. Remnants of a stone chimney that had managed to endure the years still remained, and I visualized my childhood home as it once existed, seeing myself in the past—a carefree, red-headed boy full of dreams and possibilities. It haunted me, this ghost of days gone by; yet, in the quietude, memories of my happy youth warmed my heart.

I walked a distance past the chimney to a dated well curb that was now reduced to a hip-high base of weathered stones. A heavy board covered its top, and I slid it back, peering down into a deep, dark cavity. A few ferns had taken root in the interior base of the curb and algae clung to the first few feet of the damp, rocky wall of the confining hole. Beyond that, water pooled at the bottom of the sleepy hand-dug well. Stale. Silent. An eerie calm.

I slid the board back into place and sat down on

PROLOGUE

the edge of the curb, gazing past a newer home that currently occupied the property, recalling a time long ago when I'd worked cash crops on the many acres that now lay dormant. Overwhelmed by a strong connection to the land, I then saw myself once again in the past, young and energetic, dressed in ragged overalls and carrying a fishin' pole on my way to the Big Lake. I spent a lot of my youth roaming the banks of Hurricane Creek—what we then simply called Hurrikin—and I can't help but smile remembering those happy times.

Born during the lowest point of the Great Depression, I was brought up in a family that struggled to survive the privation of the times, but with the support of surrounding relatives, we endured our hardships. We loved our land and community. Handtown, as it was then called, was home. Handtown will always be home. My old stomping grounds. No matter how far away my path in life continues to carry me, this is who I was and always will be—Georgia Boy Red—and I will forever relish the fond memories that always bring me back to the red hills of home.

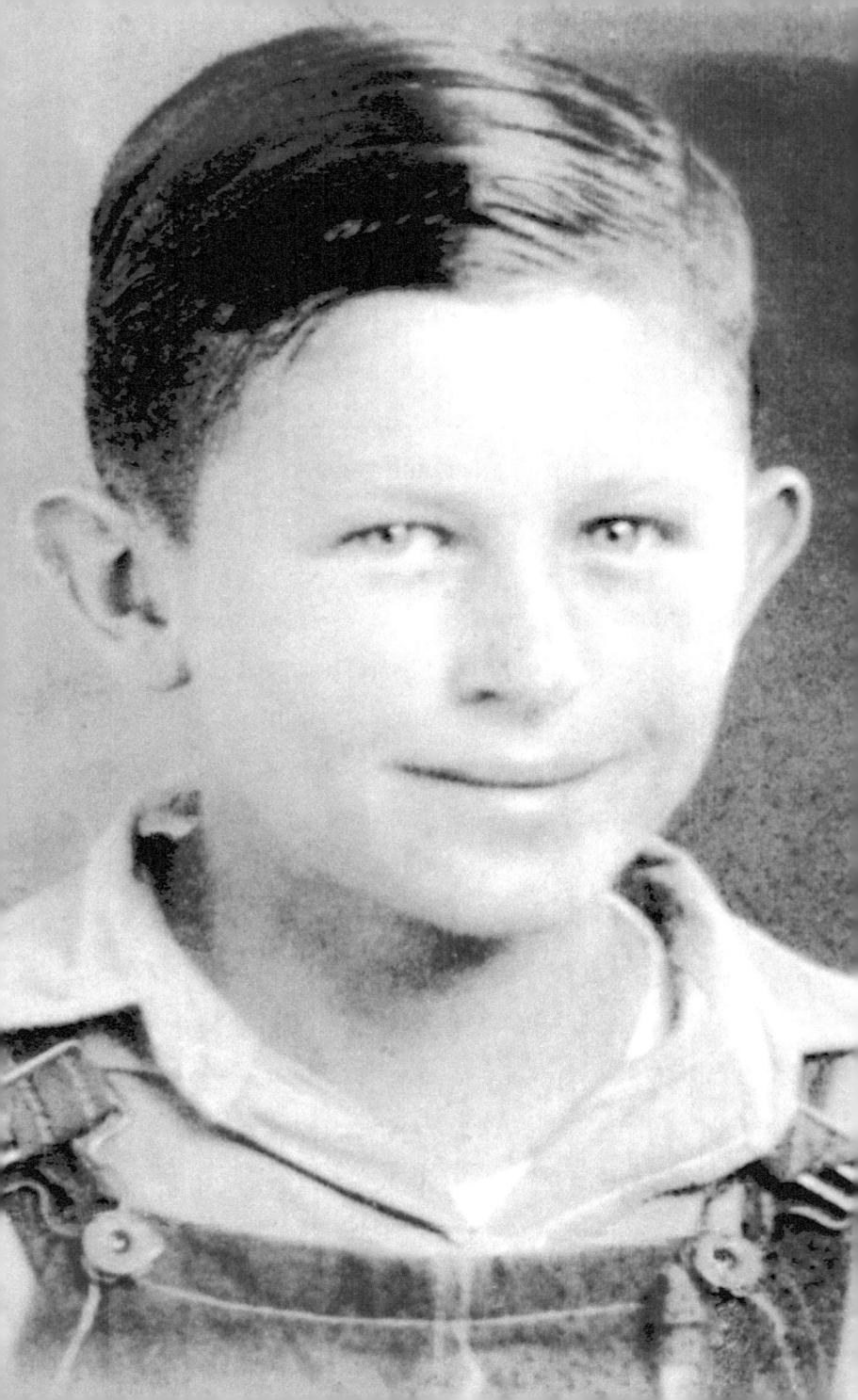

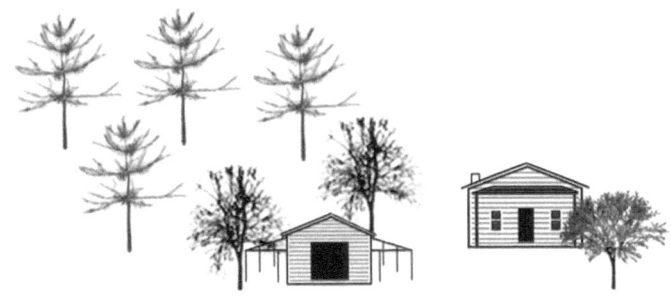

A SIMPLER PLACE & TIME

Everyone has a story to tell, and my narrative is one of a simpler place and time—the good ol' days—as seen through the eyes of a poor farm boy. Let us rewind the clock and step back in time to glimpse my humble beginnings and coming of age in the southernmost hills of Georgia, starting with a bit of history about the red hills I call home.

I was born in a rural community approximately 10 miles outside of Hazlehurst in Jeff Davis County, Georgia. The locals called the area Handtown; however, all of Hazlehurst had once been known as Handtown, named after the Hand family who were the first settlers to reside in the charming region of wooded, rolling hills and pine forests. But even before the Hands settled in that part of Southeast Georgia, the land was inhabited by the Creek, and possibly Cherokee natives. It is fertile terrain, lying a few miles southwest of where the Ocmulgee and Oconee Rivers merge into the Altamaha River, drawing an abundance of wildlife to the many rivers and streams coursing through the area known as the Three Rivers region of Southeast Georgia. Handtown was then part of Appling County, but that changed in 1905 when a new county was created from northern portions of Appling County and neighboring Coffee County, becoming the division known today as Jeff Davis County.

After the Civil War, the arrival of the railroad drastically changed the Three Rivers region, as railroad engineer Colonel George H. Hazlehurst—president of the Macon & Brunswick Railroad in 1865—began forging a rail line from Macon to Brunswick. One rail crew worked southeastward from Macon, and another crew worked northwestward from Brunswick, with the two crews eventually meeting up and connecting the lines in 1869, approximately halfway between the two cities—a spot they designated as Mile Post 8-1/2.

In 1870, with the establishment of a depot, Handtown became a rail town, offering a new mode of travel that ultimately led to the demise of the stagecoach and steamboat services, as the railroad was a much more convenient means of travel. From that time forth, Handtown was forever changed, even its name, at the request of Colonel Hazlehurst himself. But, despite the name change from Handtown to Hazlehurst, our community never broke with tradition and kept its original name alive. Holding onto roots is important; we must never forget from whence we came. For me, I am proud to call Handtown home, and you can call me Georgia Boy Red.

My parents, Warren and Nellie, owned a farm in Handtown, located along a stretch of red clay dirt road called Yawn Cemetery Road, and they grew cash crops—tobacco, corn, and cotton. We always kept a decent-sized vegetable garden (around an acre) across the road from our house, past, and to the right of our tobacco barn, in the direction of a streamlet that branched off Hurrikin (Hurricane Creek), which was located east of our farm. We raised chickens and had guinea hens, pigs, a mule, huntin' and farm dogs, and a few cows that included two dairy cows—a Jersey and a Holstein. We didn't have much money due to the economic effects of the Great Depression, and farming was our primary means of income, so we continued to raise and harvest crops, holding onto hope that the economy would soon take a turn for the better.

Necessities were often difficult to come by—farm supplies to keep up the crops, clothes, shoes—but we scraped by, learning to live on a meager allowance. Needless to say, those were hard times, but being farmers, we were able to grow our own food, get milk from our cows, eggs from our chickens, and in addition to hunting the big pine woods for wild game, we always had pork from slaughtering pigs.

Meat was cured for a week or so in our smokehouse and stored there, where I'd often stop and slice off a snack to eat when heading into the field. We also paid a grocery store in Hazlehurst to store meat for us, bartering goods as payment whenever possible. Any other meat that wasn't immediately cooked was kept by salt-curing, such as salt pork, and with any remaining pig parts, Daddy sometimes pickled hog jowls and pig feet.

Mom did her part, canning a lot of fruit and vegetables in a process of boiling glass jars, filling them with prepared food, putting on lids and bands, boiling again, and then setting them aside to cool. The lids would vacuum seal with an audible "pop" as the jars cooled down, giving us preserves such as tomatoes, corn, pickled cucumbers, peaches, watermelon rinds, and jams for all year round. Nothing tasted better than our own home-grown food. We may not have had much wealth in the monetary way, but we had our farm and family. We had each other, finding good times in the simple things life had to offer that required no money: fishing, hunting, playing music...fellowship in the company of family and friends. It was those things, and our trust in God, that saw us through and kept us going.

We lived in a little house that had been put up using lumber that was rough-sawn at the local sawmill and had never seen a lick of paint. We always called it a shotgun house 'cause there was a straight shot from front to back door. You could stand in the front doorway and look straight ahead, down a hall, and right out the back door; a bullet shot from the front door would exit right out the back door without hitting any walls. It wasn't what some folks might consider a traditional shotgun house design where one room leads directly into the next without having any hallways, but to us, the term "shotgun house" perfectly described our little house, and that's what we called it.

I was born at home (doctors made house calls in those days) in this little shotgun house on July 7, 1933. I was the pride and joy of my parents, a blue-eyed, redheaded boy whom they named Warren Jerome (I later reversed my name order and used Jerome as my first name, or simply J.W.), and courtesy of my carrottop mop, it didn't take long for me to garner the nickname Georgia Boy Red. I was the first of what would eventually become four children, remaining the only child for two and a half years. That was when my sister, Shirley, came along, and life, after her arrival, was never the same.

My mother took care of the house and helped run the farm. She was a good-natured, Christian woman, tall and slender, with dark hair that she'd typically pin back. She sewed her own clothes, mainly modest midcalf-length dresses, which was how most women in Handtown dressed at that time. Attire was practical and suited for everyday wear, what folks could afford during the Depression era.

Mom was very talented and loved music. She had a mandolin that her parents had bought for her when she was young that she'd learned to play at an early age. It was a pretty mandolin, a real nice one, and when she picked those strings, she made that instrument sing in true bluegrass fashion. You couldn't help but do a little flatfoot backsteppin' when she played. That was the South Georgia sound—fiddles, guitars, banjos, and mandolins—a true southern pastime.

When I was around three years old—according to what Mom and Daddy had always told me—I did a terrible thing to that mandolin she'd loved so much. I was walkin' around with a quart jar of water (that's about all we drank out of, quart and pint mason jars), and

Mom's mandolin was lyin' on a chair. Well, I poured that full jar of water right in the sound hole of that mandolin, drenchin' the inside of her much-loved instrument. Even though I was young, I do have a faint recollection of that moment, probably due to Mom's reaction to me ruinin' something that meant so much to her.

"Boy was she mad," Daddy told me years later. "I don't think I'd ever seen her so mad."

According to Daddy, she immediately grabbed the mandolin up, flipped it over, doing all she could to dry it out in a desperate attempt to save it, but the damage was done. The interior unfinished wood had swelled, causing the mandolin to warp, and knowing it was my fault, my heart weighed heavy with guilt.

At that young age, I had no idea the damage that pouring water into a wooden instrument could cause, and I don't really know why I did it. In all fairness, I was just a little boy, holding a glass of water, looking for someplace to pour it. I just so happened to have chosen the most unfortunate of places. It all added up to this: little boy + jar full of water + hole to pour it in = trouble.

That pretty much summed it up.

Despite the damage I'd caused to that instrument, Mom continued to play her warped mandolin for many years to come, until a future time when she'd finally gotten a new one. Even then, she'd take out that old mandolin and pick those strings, recalling the day her parents had given it to her, as well as the day I'd ruined it by fillin' the sound hole with water—bittersweet memories.

When I was a little older, Mom still brought up that mandolin story on occasion, even sharing it with the entire congregation of the Philadelphia Baptist Church, where we attended services. The church was just a mile or so north of our house, a small frame building that had been constructed in 1900 and was in dire need of being rebuilt to meet the needs of the congregation. Behind the church lay a cemetery cradled by woods, a peaceful, tranquil restin' place that fit with the welcoming feel of the church. There was only one thing missin' that would have made the experience of attending services there all the better, and that was restrooms. Of course, churches without restrooms were not uncommon in those days, and the congregation dealt with the issue by designating two separate areas of woods for privacy between the women and men. To do one's business, the women had the accommodation of an outhouse in their area, but I don't recall the men having had any such convenience, leaving the fellas to simply make do with nature. However, with the mention of outhouses, let me share this tidbit of humor:

> If using an outhouse, please keep in mind
> Within that hole you might just find
> A creepin' critter of the slitherin' kind
> So, you'd best beware of your bare behind

During the late 1930s, most folks owned automobiles, but with precious little money to purchase gasoline, many families continued to drive a horse and wagon wherever possible within our farming community. For us, that meant hitchin' our mule, Emer, to our wagon for many of our trips to and from church, where Daddy took an active role serving as the Sunday school superintendent, and Mom played her mandolin.

We always considered the Philadelphia Baptist Church to be our home church, but now and again, Mom would visit a Church of God located approximately four miles north of the Baptist church, where one of her sisters attended. It was a holiness Pentecostal church with members often getting touched by the Holy Ghost, and when the spirit moved, the people moved—running, shoutin', and speaking in tongues.

Despite Mom's occasional visits to the Church of God, Daddy always remained a steadfast devotee of the Philadelphia Baptist Church, the only church he and Mom were ever members of in those days. Pastor Ledford was the preacher of our little church that played a major role in our lives. He was an energetic, young minister, well-liked, but often long-winded. His sermons were lengthy, frequently leading to a few nodding heads before he was done, but he preached the gospel truth according to the teachings of the Bible and led his close-nit Christian flock to follow the narrow road. For as said in Matthew 7:14, "Because strait is the gate, and narrow is the way, which leadeth unto life, and few there be that find it."

Once a year the church would have a big homecoming event with dinner on the ground and singin'. Following Sunday morning service, tables would be set up and loaded with food, where flies shared in the bounty, lickin' up the juices of fried chicken, ham, purple hulls, chicken n' dumplings, and all things southernly delicious, including all of those homemade cakes, pies, and cobblers. There were always plenty of dessert staples to go around, with my favorites being coconut cake and pecan pie. Dinner on the ground was always a feast, then after we'd filled our bellies, we'd make our way back inside the church for an hour or two of old-timey southern gospel sounds before packing up and callin' it a day.

Through the years, Mom had told me a few stories of things I'd done as a small boy, but I don't remember much of my preschool days. I do, however, remember my first tricycle. Friends and family had gathered at our house one evening for a peanut boilin' get-together—something we did quite often during peanut season. At that party, Daddy and Mom surprised me with a little tricycle that someone had brought them to give to me. I was so excited to get it, and I rode that tricycle through our shotgun house, back and forth from front to back door, over and over again.

That evening, one of my uncles from my dad's side of the family kept tellin' me to see how fast I could go, urging me to pedal faster and faster. So, listening to him, I set a starting point at the front door and pedaled as hard as I could toward the open back door, only to find that I couldn't stop. Like a daredevil, I barreled out the door, sailed across the peeling planked porch, and took a steep dive to the ground. I came up cryin', suffering only a few bruises, but seein' my uncle's amusement and knowing he was having a good laugh at my expense left my feelings more bruised than my body. Even to this day, I can still hear his big, booming laugh, reminding me of an important lesson I'd learned that night: Don't do everything someone might tell you to do, especially if that someone was my loving uncle whom I shall not name.

Life went on as usual on the farm. There were a lot of daily chores, and before long, I was big enough to start helping Daddy feed the livestock, slop the pigs, milk the cows, weed the vegetable garden, and gather eggs that the chickens had laid. Our crib barn stood in front of the house, on the northwest corner, a small barn that had lean-to shed roof extensions on three sides that incorporated covered stalls. A decent-sized enclosure stretched across the front of the barn that connected to stalls on the east side of the building, where we kept our mule. We'd let Emer and the cows out in the field during the day to graze, and we'd bring 'em back in at night when we fed them. Inside the building, we kept the bottom crib full of corn—everyone and everything on the farm ate corn—and in the loft, we stored hay for winter—peanut hay and millet, among other sources. A chicken coop sat behind the house, near the outhouse, and just in front of it, on the southeast side, was our well, about 40 feet from our back door. Being tobacco farmers, we had a tobacco barn—around 20 feet tall, built by Daddy from hewn pine logs he'd cut down on our land, and sealed with daubing—situated across from our crib barn, on the opposite side of Yawn Cemetery, where our property extended into pine woods in the westerly direction. It was a good-sized farm, around 86 acres of largely wooded land—aside from the 18 acres Daddy had cleared for farming, later telling me how he'd removed the many large tree stumps by boring a hole under each one and blowin' 'em out of the ground with half-stick dynamite. He plowed and planted crops on those 18 acres, with the remainder of the property left wooded, and Daddy was proud to say he owned his land free and clear. The farm was wholly ours, and it was home.

THE EARLY YEARS

Holidays in Handtown typically meant another big dinner at church, as our church was our social center, and congregations celebrated holidays together. Most everyone in Handtown attended the Philadelphia Baptist Church—some regularly and others occasionally—and for me, that included a lot of my great many relatives scattered about the area. When I was little, church is where I remember having had our main Thanksgiving celebrations, but Mom would also cook up something special for home, such as a delicious pot of chicken n' dumplings, a meal we usually made on special occasions. I don't have any memories of her ever cookin' a turkey—wild turkey populations were at a decline during that time—for our holiday meals, and I think I would have remembered if she had. I do, however, recall her preparing a hen and making chicken n' dressing from homemade cornbread cooked in a pan on her cast iron wood-burning stove—a cooker that had four burner plates and incorporated an oven—heated by filling its firebox with chopped stove wood that we kept stacked on our back porch. Thinking back, I hanker after that chicken n' dressing—a dish I could never get enough of.

Moving into Christmastime, Mom and Daddy always did their best to make the holiday special, not letting the hardships of those Depression-era days dampen their spirit. Before Christmas, we'd all go out into the woods and cut down a pine tree. We'd take it home and decorate it with little things we'd make. On Christmas Eve night, we'd gather around the fireplace, and Mom and Daddy would give me and Shirley stockings—Mom's old, worn-out stockings that she'd cut and fill with the likes of an apple, an orange, a tangerine, and a little bit of candy. We'd always get some kind of small toy and maybe an article of clothing. I remember getting a shirt one year, along with a little car that I'd spent many hours playin' with outside, inexpensive gifts that held little monetary value, but the day was no less magical for it.

Even though we opened gifts on Christmas Eve, we still enjoyed the fun associated with the notion of Santa Claus. One Sunday before Christmas, we were at church when Santa came parading through the door and up the aisle to the tune of "Here Comes Santa Claus", walking toward the pulpit with a big sack flung over his shoulder.

"Ho, ho, ho." He laughed, and his belly shook. "Merry Christmas!"

Mrs. Claus was with him, only she wasn't a very feminine Mrs. Claus, seein' as it was my cousin Watson wearing a wig and dress playin' the part of Santa's wife. It made for a fun, memorable night, though, with his comical performance giving everyone a good laugh.

On Christmas day we enjoyed the gifts we'd

THE EARLY YEARS

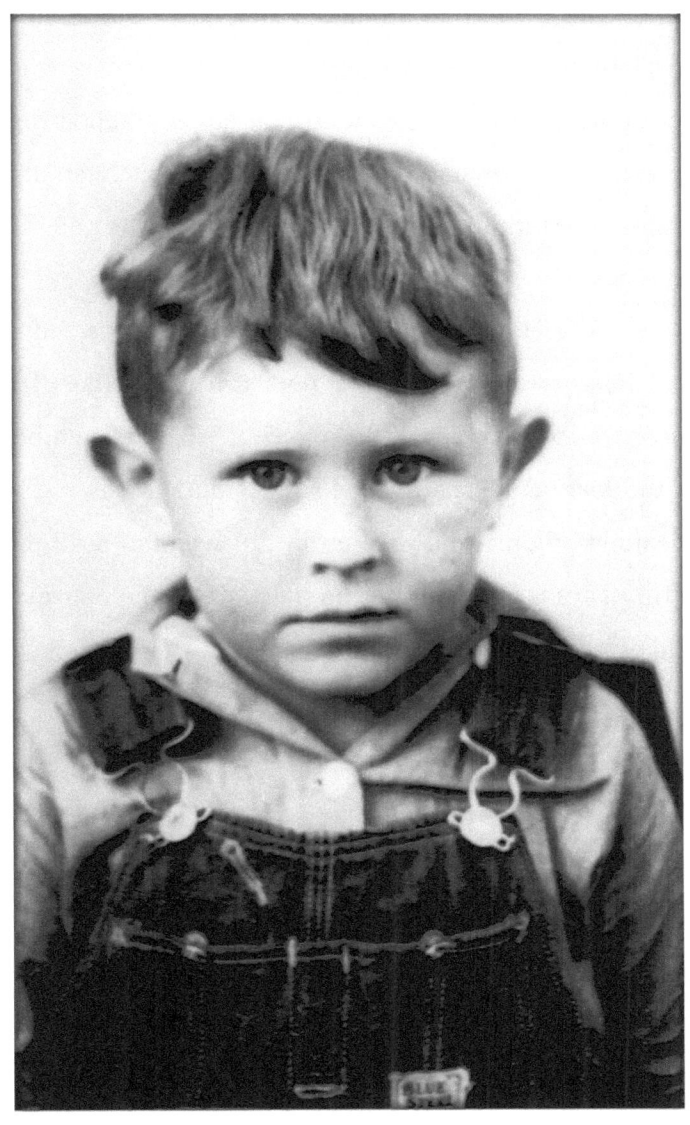

gotten the night before while Mom cooked a holiday meal much the same as what we'd had on Thanksgiving, filling the house with a wonderful bouquet of tantalizing aromas. Our holiday feasts may not have been the grandest in the county, but they were thoroughly enjoyed.

We didn't have much at Christmastime, but I had been taught from the time I can remember that there was so much more to rejoice in every December 25th than gifts, big dinners, or Santa, for the true meaning of Christmas resides in the celebration of the birth of Jesus Christ, found in the story of the nativity—Luke 2:1-20.

* * * *

UNCLE THOMAS AND AUNT ARTHA—one of my daddy's brothers and his wife—lived nearby our farm on Yawn Cemetery Road, just on the next hill. They had a big white house with a front porch, and across the road, to the left and behind their crib barn, stood a tall tobacco barn with an attached lean-to shed roof supported by posts. One day, while Daddy, Mom, and I were at their house for a visit, I slipped away from Mom and sneaked out to the barn, where Daddy, Uncle Thomas, and their brother Hamp were working on an old car beneath the open-sided shed roof. Daddy, dressed in trousers with suspenders and wearing a blue, long-sleeve button-down shirt, was sporting a newsboy cap. He had one foot propped up on the fender of the car, laughing at something one of my uncles had said. They weren't aware I was there, and I slipped past them and climbed up on that high shed roof, recklessly walking across the tin till reaching a point directly above them. Peering down through a wide gap where part of the metal roof was missing, I suddenly lost my footing and fell through the gap, landing right on top of that old car they were working on, scaring the daylights out of all three of them.

"Red!" Daddy looked up at the hole in the roof, momentarily stunned by his son falling from the sky. "What on earth were—" He stopped yelling when he saw I was bleeding from a considerable gash above my left eye. "Son, you're hurt."

"It looks bad." Uncle Hamp scooped me up and rushed to the house with Daddy and Uncle Thomas trailing close behind.

By that time, the front of my overalls was covered in blood, and when Mom saw me, she panicked. "We need to get him to the doctor."

Aunt Artha got some damp towels and handed them to Daddy. He pressed one against the laceration and started cleaning me up to see how bad it was. "It's deep, but the bleeding's slowin' down."

"Did he break anything?" Uncle Thomas checked my arms and legs for any swelling or injuries, finding none.

"I think he's gonna be okay." Daddy was too relieved to be mad.

"That was one long drop. And he landed smack-dab on the car." Uncle Hamp was amazed. "God's certainly lookin' out for you, Red, by cushioning your fall."

"Amen," the others agreed.

Other than that gash that eventually healed and left a scar above my left eye, I had walked away from that fall practically unscathed, and life went on as usual.

My parents spent a lot of time with Uncle Thomas and Aunt Artha, but I had numerous relatives that lived in and around Hazlehurst from both sides of the family. My daddy, on his side alone, was one of twelve children, and that made for a lot of aunts, uncles, and cousins.

My granddad and grandma (my daddy's parents) also owned a farm along Yawn Cemetery, a little farther south, past Uncle Thomas and Aunt Artha's place, where Yawn Cemetery intersected with Post Rd. They had a sizable farm, with land spanning both sides of Yawn Cemetery Road, with their homestead nestled close to a small cemetery for which the road was named. They had a nice, big house with a wide front porch, only they had no indoor kitchen and had to do all of their cookin' and eatin' in a separate building that stood behind their house.

I spent a lot of time with my granddad, mostly fishing, his favorite thing to do. He used to take me and my first cousin Judon—his mom and my daddy were siblings—fishin' with him to a widened area of Hurrikin

(Hurricane Creek) that we called the Big Lake. From the root-laden banks of the amber waters that twined through the surrounding woods, there were several expanded areas along Hurrikin, but this particular spot—the Big Lake—was the widest point, and the best location for fishing. This is where Granddad taught me and Judon how to catch small brim, put a hook in 'em, and throw them out in the deep water with a cork on the line to catch the big fish in the lake, always hoping for a good-sized bass.

Granddad loved the lake, chewing and spittin' tobacco while lazin' around waiting for a fish to bite, fully appreciating the peaceful and relaxing atmosphere, and the thrill of catchin' those fish. He'd take 'em home, clean 'em, and put 'em on the table for the rest of us to enjoy, but oddly enough, he never ate any of the fish we caught. He didn't like fish. I never saw him take a bite of one, but that didn't stop him from going down to the Big Lake that he loved so much and catching them for the rest of us to enjoy eatin'. He was happy to do it, 'cause fishin' made him happy.

Granddad was one of the most self-sufficient

men I knew, always seeming to have a practical solution to any problem, and that included dealing with unpredictable afternoon thunderstorms. Many times we'd be out on Hurrikin, way down at the Big Lake fishin', and a storm would roll in. Granddad would hear thunder and see the dark clouds gathering, and he'd say, "Come on boys," and he'd take me and Judon to an old hollow tree that was just big enough to house both of us. He'd place us inside that hollow to keep us dry, and he'd instruct us to stay there till he came back after the skies cleared, leaving us tucked up in that ol' hollow tree to ride out the storm. I never doubted Granddad, and just as he always assured us, as soon as the rain stopped, he'd return straight away to get us, completely dry and ready to go back fishin'. He knew that land better than anyone in Handtown, and he knew right where all of those old hollowed-out trees stood. So, as long as a few creepy-crawlies didn't bother you, there was always shelter from the storms.

The RED HILLS of HOME

* * * *

IT WAS HOT IN JULY in South Georgia. Mid-afternoon temperatures were miserable, with the heat only relieved by blessed afternoon showers. Those were the dog days of summer, the time of year when the sweet smell of ripening tobacco crops neared harvest, and you could hardly stand the sticky heat.

We had no electricity or running water inside our house, so when we needed water, we had to draw it out of the well with a bucket that we utilized by use of a simple fixed (single) pulley system that raised it up and down. In the summertime, when we needed to bathe, we'd usually go down to the creek on those hot days, jump in, and take a bath down there. In the wintertime, though, we'd often take our baths in a tub at the house. We'd draw water from the well, and Mom would boil it and fill the tubs on our back porch with hot water. We had a #2 and a #3 tub. The #2 tub was smaller, and when we kids were little, that's the one we used to take our baths in.

With no indoor plumbing in those days, using

an outhouse was also customary. There was no toilet paper for wiping, so we kept plenty of mail-order Montgomery Ward and Sears Roebuck catalogs on hand, always stacking a couple on either side of the seat for easy reach. You'd just tear out one of the slick pages and wipe. That's simply how it was done. Times were simple, often inconvenient, but living with those inconveniences was the normal way of living at that time.

Mom had her hands full keepin' house, tending to me and Shirley, and helping out on the farm. Doing laundry was quite a chore in and of itself. On laundry days (usually once a week), Mom would fill three metal tubs with water, one for washing with a washboard, and the other two for rinsing. She'd scrub the clothes with soap using the washboard, wring them, and then, if washing a load of whites or heavily soiled clothes, she'd boil them in a big, three-legged cast iron boiling pot that sat by our smokehouse, near the well. Next, using the two rinse tubs, she'd transfer them to tub one to rinse and wring, then repeat in tub two. If washing white clothes, she might add bluing to the first rinse, and any starch was added before hanging the clothes on the clothesline in our back yard.

That was the basic routine, but I even recall seeing Mom lay clothing on an old stump and beat them with a wooden paddle to get the dirt out before rinsing and wringing. Laundry was an arduous job, and she washed clothes like that for many years. She worked hard, but she got a little assistance when her mother, my Grandma Persons, came to live with us and stayed for several years.

Grandma Persons looked after me and Shirley, and she liked me really well. She didn't punish me too much, getting after Shirley more than she did me, but when Shirley and I didn't mind her, or got quarreling, she'd chase after us, and we'd run. She'd chase us 'round the old red-brick well curb in the back yard, her apron flappin', fiercely wagging an index finger in reprimand—a chase we'd keep up until she got dizzy or wore herself out.

Getting under the bed was always a good option for escape, but when Shirley attempted that tactic, I remember Grandma Persons crawling down there and whippin' her from the side of the bed, allowing me to escape outside. Grandma's spankings really weren't all that bad, though, and running from her really became more of a game—keep away from Grandma Persons. Of course, I wasn't the one gettin' most of those spankings, that was little sis, leaving me to believe that I was either Grandma Person's favorite, or if truth be told, just a little better at the game.

These are some of my earliest memories of life in the 1930s for a southern Georgia boy from a little community called Handtown. Humble and uncomplicated, naïve to the enormity of the world beyond those red hills of home, but I had quite some start, and this was just the beginning.

ALL FORGIVEN

In 1939, at the age of six, the time had come for me to start school, and I sure didn't want to go. My school was in Denton, about eight miles from our house, give or take a mile or two, and Mom and Daddy had to put me on that school bus kickin' and screamin'. I sure made a spectacle of us all for the first few days, but I eventually came to accept the fact that I had to go, much as I certainly didn't want to.

I carried my lunch in a gallon-size syrup bucket. Mom would pack bread or crackers with a couple of other things like biscuits, sausage, boiled eggs, a little syrup in a container, an apple if we could get it, and depending on the season, maybe seasonal fruit, peanuts, or pecans. I usually had a pint jar of water to drink, always happy to get whatever she packed, knowing I was lucky to have it.

I hadn't been in school long, when in September, the threat of a second world war loomed over our family with news broadcast that Germany had invaded Poland, prompting declarations of war by France and the United Kingdom. Folks could barely make ends meet, still struggling from the lingering effects of the Great Depression, and now the worry of a second bloody war weighed heavily on everyone's minds.

"I hope no one gets drafted," Daddy fretted. "The last thing we need is another war like the last." He looked at me. "When you get a little older, I'll tell you about World War I. I was a boy then. About your same age."

Daddy didn't like the idea of war, something I didn't mentally grasp at the young age of six. I didn't comprehend the gravity of what war meant, but I recall the tension that seized our family during that worrisome time, unbeknownst to us that in just two short years—after an attack on Pearl Harbor—the United States would be drawn into what had become the second world war. And just as Daddy had earlier feared, men were soon drafted under the nation's first peacetime draft in 1940—the Selective Service and Training Act—that initially required men between the ages of 21 and 35 to register for military service; however, after the attack on Pearl Harbor and declaration of war by the United States on Japan, the age requirement was expanded to between the ages of 18 and 65.

I remember Daddy talking about all of the men that voluntarily enlisted after the attack on Pearl Harbor, but those that did not volunteer were subject to the national lottery, and if drafted, were required to serve on active duty for 12 months, followed by 10 years (or up to the age of 45) in the reserves. The draft affected most families in some manner, including ours, with one of my cousins being called into service. It was a call of duty that he had no choice but to answer, leaving the family to worry, wait, and pray for his safe return.

The draft was especially hard on farming families who relied on these young men to keep their farms afloat. Times were trying, but in our little corner of the world, farm life went on, and we put our trust in God and made the best of it. By the time I had turned seven that year, our family had grown to a household of four, with the addition of another sibling. I then had a six-month-old brother, Ronald, who had been born in January of 1940, making him six-and-a-half years my junior. I was glad to have a brother, and like me, he was another freckle-faced redhead, and I was more than happy to share that spotlight.

I still hated attending school, as I didn't do well in class and often got picked on due to bein' a freckle-faced redhead, but luckily, I had a cousin named Winnette who helped me out. Her dad, my Uncle Clifton, was married to one of my daddy's sisters, Winnie, and they owned a store and sold gas a mile or so west of our homestead, on Taylor Road. There was, in fact, two stores on Taylor Road, the second being a country grocery owned by Tommy and Missie Wilcox that was located a little farther south of Uncle Clifton's store, at the corner of Post and Taylor.

On schoolday mornings, Winnette would often walk a trail that ran through the woods between their farm and ours to catch the bus with me, just to make sure I went to school. Thinking back, I probably had Aunt Winnie to thank for Winnette looking after me, as my aunt was like a second mother; she was very good to me and treated me just like one of her own kids.

Even though Winnette was only a year older than me, she'd get me on the bus and see that I got to class, checking on her little blue-eyed, carrottop cousin whenever possible. She and I had a very good friendship, but she was also subject to my occasional tantrums. She was well aware that I had a bit of a temper that accompanied being a carrottop, for which I didn't like being teased, and one day, while we were playing outside, she said something that flared my temper. She knew me well, and she knew to run, but while she was attempting to climb over our hog wire fence in escape, I bit her right on the butt, leaving her with a permanent mark that she reminded me of many years later.

Afterwards, all was forgiven, but I'd felt terrible

for what I'd done and never bit her again. Despite the incident, we remained fast friends, and she continued to look after me. She knew how much I hated school, and thanks to her, those schoolday mornings were much more bearable.

Three years later, in July of 1943, WW2 still loomed as I reached the age of ten. At that time, rubber, gasoline, kerosene, shoes, meats, coffee, and sugar, among other things, had been rationed and could only be purchased with ration stamps. Every household was issued ration books, and rationed items could not be purchased without an accompanying stamp. Although sugar was hard to come by, we managed to get our hands on some from a man who raised bees and had several beehives in our area. In exchange for honey, the government would provide him sugar to feed the bees in his many beehives he had scattered around the state, and when he was in our vicinity, we would get sugar from him.

We didn't go into town very often, Daddy went whenever necessary, and we'd make family trips once or twice a year. A grocery truck would come 'round the rural farmsteads once a month, and we'd buy what we needed. Ice was also delivered every month, and we'd buy 300 pounds each time, which we stored in a 3-foot-deep hole in the ground of our smokehouse, keeping it fully enveloped in sawdust. It usually kept the whole month long, and when we needed ice for our tea, which we drank daily, we'd go out to the smokehouse, scoop back the sawdust, and chip some off.

Mom and Daddy were accustomed to scrimping and making do with what they had, and nothing went to waste. Mom did a lot of sewing, and she used to make flour sack dresses for Shirley and shirts for me and Ronald. Making clothing and household items out of flour and feed sacks was something women had been doing since before the Great Depression. The sacks were a popular source of cotton fabric and came in an array of bright colors and assorted prints specifically made for the purpose of being reused for clothing. Mom would sit at her old treadle sewing machine with Shirley often working the pedal, and she'd transform those cotton flour sacks into clothing worthy of being donned.

Mom took care of many tasks around the farm, with some chores more laborious than others. We used to have a large, three-legged cast iron boiling pot by our smokehouse, near the well, and Mom would light a fire under it and use it for multiple purposes such as washing clothes, boiling peanuts, making lye soap, and boiling hogs we'd slaughtered, which is how we'd rake the hair off 'em. Sometimes she'd get the fire going so high that it would spread out of control, and she'd go to jumpin' around that pot and stompin' at the flames, trying to put it out. She'd panic and race for the well to get water to douse it.

One day, while watching her in just such a predicament, I ran and found some paint and a brush and wrote a little poem about her on the well curb. Using her first and middle name, I wrote:

> Nellie Scott
> Jumped in the pot
> It got so hot
> She had to trot

Thinking back to what I'd written, I actually should have written:

> Nellie Scott
> Jumped 'round the pot
> It got so hot
> She had to trot

I thought it was funny, but Mom, of course, wasn't too amused. Over time, though, seein' as it took years for the paint to wear away, she eventually came to find the humor in it.

By that time in my life, I had matured enough that Daddy had taught me how to hunt and trap game in the woods surrounding our farm. He always kept two or three huntin' dogs for fox hunting, but we also did a lot of coon huntin', as we could sell 'em for a little money. We never wasted meat, eating nearly anything we shot, with the exception of raccoons. We did, however, eat possum, only after keeping them in a big, round barrel for two weeks and feeding them good to clean them out, and we also ate rabbits, quail, deer, and sometimes, even squirrels.

I once found a baby gray squirrel that had fallen out of its nest, a tiny, little thing that I scooped up, took home, and milk fed. I managed to keep him alive, and before long, he grew up and made a big, healthy squirrel. He'd ride on my shoulder, and I considered him a pet, but I never put him in a cage, allowing him to come and go as he pleased.

One day, one of my mom's sisters had come for a visit, along with her husband and some of their eight children, a couple of which were more than ten years my senior. I'm not certain which of my cousins had visited that day, except for Hazel, and I recall her for one very specific reason—Squirrel's tail yank, and my throbbing finger.

We, kids, were out in the yard carryin' on and cuttin' up while the grownups talked inside the house. I had my squirrel—I just called him Squirrel—with me, riding on my shoulder as he typically did, and I was having a good time with my cousins until Hazel suddenly ran up behind me, grabbed poor little Squirrel by the tail, and gave a quick yank that scared him awful.

I was petting him at the time, and he bit a hole straight through my finger with his little razor-sharp teeth before leaping off my shoulder and running for the trees. I tried to catch him, but he scooted down the hill toward Uncle Thomas's place and disappeared in the pines and underbrush, where I couldn't find him. He was gone.

Lying in bed that night with a throbbing finger, I stared up at the rafters, spotting a rat snake slithering through the open, overhead space. The walls and ceiling of our farmhouse were never finished, just exposed studs, leaving plenty of gaps for critters to squeeze through, and it was up in those open rafters where Squirrel would go at night while I slept. I looked for him every night for some time to come, but he never came back. I was so mad at Hazel, 'cause thanks to her, I never saw Squirrel again. I really loved my furry little buddy, but I understood that she never intended any harm, and after a while, all was forgiven.

The RED HILLS of HOME

* * * *

GRANDMA HAD A BEAUTIFUL ARBOR behind her house that was covered in mature grape vines, and every fall it was loaded with ripe grapes. She loved that arbor and always warned the kids to stay off of it; but, of course, that didn't stop me and Judon from climbing up on it one fine autumn day and pickin' her grapes. We didn't think Grandma had seen us slip around her house and thought we were in the clear, but when we spotted her sneaking up on us from behind the smokehouse, we knew we were in serious trouble.

"What are you doin' up there." She ran toward us with a broom in her hand and started jabbing us with the wooden handle. "I told you not to get on my grapevines. You get off them right now." She kept jabbing us from underneath the arbor, and not in a gentle way. "You know you're gonna ruin it. Get down from there." She poked harder and harder with that broomstick, determined to teach us a lesson.

"Ow!" I scrambled for the edge of the arbor.

"Ow, ow, ow!" Judon scrambled off the other

end.

When our feet hit the ground, we tore off runnin' with Grandma still after us, swinging that straw broom with a vengeance.

"She sure was mad," Judon said, when we'd finally stopped running.

"Yeah, we'd better stay off her grapevines." I licked the tips of my fingers that were sticky from grape juice, a taste so good that the temptation of seeing those ripe grapes was simply too hard to resist.

I didn't visit Grandma and Granddad for a few days after that, but when I did go back, all was forgiven; that is, with another firm reminder from Grandma to stay off her grapevine arbor.

BAD EXPERIENCES

Shirley used to pretend play in a house of make-believe, and Ronald and I, being the typical boys we were, loved to get her riled by messing up her playtime. One day, to get away from the aggravation, she decided to carry some boards up into the old chinaberry tree that stood in our front yard, where she set up house. She lugged several cored bricks up in that tree and filled the holes with berries she'd picked off the branches, pretending she was cookin' a delicious supper with the berries being chicken, potatoes, pie....

Having nothing better to do at the time, I climbed up in the chinaberry tree while she played in make-believe land, exploring the higher limbs, leaving Ronald strugglin' to climb up to the lowest limb below us. We were having fun, and everything was hunky-dory until Shirley accidentally dropped a brick that hurled down and struck Ronald on the head, knocking him out of the tree. Unable to do anything, I gasped, hearing him hit the ground with a thud.

"Mom!" I called out while scrambling down the tree as fast as I could.

After catching his breath that had been knocked out of him, Ronald cried out, and Mom came running. She scooped him up, carried him over to a swing that hung from the rafters of our front porch, and inspected him for injuries.

"Red, run inside and get me a wet rag," she told me.

I hurried into the house and returned with a cool, damp rag that Mom pressed against a gash that was bleeding above Ronald's left eye, high up on his forehead and into his hairline.

"He needs to see a doctor." Mom was worried. "Shirley, since your dad's not here, I need you to run over to Thomas and Artha's place and get someone to drive us to see a doctor."

Shirley tore off runnin' for the next hill, and I stayed to help Mom. While we waited, she held Ronald in her lap and cradled him tight in her arms. She prayed, and then she softly sang as they rocked on that porch swing for what felt like an eternity before our ride finally arrived.

Thankfully, Ronald was not badly hurt, but it was a scary moment that reminded me of the time I had fallen from the lean-to shed roof of Uncle Thomas's tobacco barn when I was a tyke. Today, I realize how lucky my brother and I truly were to have walked away from our accidents with no serious injuries. I give thanks to our guardian angels who continue to keep us in their watch, knowing we haven't always made their jobs easy.

Psalm 91:11

"For he shall give his angels charge over thee, to keep thee in all thy ways."

BAD EXPERIENCES

Round about that time, I'd developed an interest in learning to play an instrument, so Mom started teaching me to play her mandolin, planning for us to pick and sing together at church. I practiced learning the chords, and in a short time, I was playin' better than expected.

One evening, our church was having a reunion, and Mom and I had been asked to sing a couple of songs. Wanting me to look nice, she made me dress up in a little fancy suit, and she was so proud of how I looked. Unfortunately, I didn't stay looking good for long, 'cause I got to running around the woods outside the church with some of the boys and ended up in a fight, rollin' around on the ground, getting my little fancy suit all dirty and rumpled.

"Red," I heard Mom call, and the boys took off running.

I hadn't expected Mom to come outside looking for me, and when she saw me, boy, did she get mad.

"Look what you've done to your clothes." She grabbed my arm. "We're supposed to sing."

She dragged me to the front door of the church,

marched me up the aisle, and plopped me down on the front pew for all the congregation to see. I knew I looked a mess and was aware of everyone staring, and when the preacher called on Mom to sing, she made me get up in front of all those people—a few of whom were laughing—handed me the mandolin, and we sang our songs.

Today, picturing how I must have looked standing up there with my face smudged with dirt, my hair mussed, and wearing a rumpled suit all covered in red dust, I can't help but laugh. It was not one of my best experiences, but I played my heart out, knowing how much singin' that night meant to Mom. Yet, despite what I'd done, everything worked out fine, and the congregation thoroughly enjoyed our songs.

* * * *

I HAD AN AUNT who stayed with us for a while, and the thing I remember most about her was her snuff habit. She didn't sniff it, though, she dipped it. My first cousin and I would watch her pull out her bottom lip, hold the can up, and tap the powdery tobacco into her mouth with fine-tuned precision. Every so often, she might scoop out a pinch with her fingers, but being the seasoned user she was, she was an expert with her technique of tapping it loose without having to get her fingers dirty.

One day, my cousin said, "Get us some of her snuff, and we'll try it."

Going along with his plan, I sneaked a can of her Copenhagen that was about ¾ full and slipped it out of the house. Eager to try it, we headed way down in the field, alongside a back road, where no one would catch us with the stolen snuff.

I held the can out to my cousin. "You try it first, then I will."

He shook his head and said, "No, you try it, then I'll try it."

We kept this exchange up, going back and forth for quite a while, until I finally said, "Okay, I'll try it."

I had watched my aunt put the snuff in her mouth many times, and so I attempted to do it the same way I'd always seen her do it. I pulled out my bottom lip, tipped the can up, and shook it, but instead of a small amount shaking loose, nearly all of the remaining snuff fell out at one time and covered my face. It went in my mouth, up my nose, and in my eyes. I couldn't help swallowing some, and in a panic, I flailed about trying to catch my breath. I gagged. I hacked. I spit and spit and spit, thinking I might die. Needless-to-say, that was my one and only time ever dipping snuff.

After I finally got straightened out and was able to say something, I looked at my cousin and said, "There's a little left. Now, it's your turn."

After witnessing my bad experience, he chickened out and tore off runnin' across the field, getting away from me—and the last of the snuff—as fast as he could. Luckily for him, I was still too out of sorts to chase him down.

I had another aunt—my mom had several sisters—that lived with her husband and two sons in Douglas, and one day they drove out to see us. During their visit, Mom and Daddy planned for me to go and stay with them for a week or so, to pick cotton, with my uncle agreeing to pay me a certain amount per pound to do the job. I was then around the age of ten, and I'd

done a good deal of pickin' cotton on our own farm and knew how to get the job done, precisely what my uncle was counting on.

In the fall, when the cotton crops were ready to harvest, there was nothing like the sight of cotton blanketing a field white. But pickin' cotton in the South Georgia heat was laborious, not quite as bad as cropping tobacco leaves, as I hated getting covered in sap from lugging those bundles of leaves under my arms, but it was tiring pickin' cotton and filling those burlap or old feed bags from sunup till sundown, being careful not to cut up my hands on the bolls. I also had never been away from home before, and I wasn't too keen on the idea, but it had already been decided for me to go, so I packed a bag for my time away.

My first night at their farm in Douglas, I was given a place to sleep on the floor, as they had no extra beds. I climbed under a quilt and stared up at the ceiling, missing home and my own bed, feeling worse by the minute. I hated my situation and wanted to go home, feeling that my family was a million miles away. I felt tears building, and I tried not to cry, but I couldn't help it, and soon everyone heard my embarrassing display.

"Woman." My uncle talked through his nose. "Can't you do somethin' with that boy?" His twangy voice rang out. "Hush him up, or we'll never get any sleep. You need to do somethin' with him."

Hearing my uncle complain only made my crying worse.

"I ain't puttin' up with this." He grumbled. "We're sending that boy home."

I tried to quiet down, but I didn't want to be there for even that one night, much less for a full week. My aunt and uncle were great folks, but that night, it was clear as day that I wasn't ready to be away from home. I don't know how long I cried or when I finally drifted off to sleep, but come morning light, my aunt sent a letter by mail to Mom and Daddy that they were sending me home the next day.

After enduring a second night of homesickness, they put me on a train from Douglas to Denton, where Mom and Daddy were told in the note to pick me up at the station, but when I got off the train in Denton, no one was there to meet me. I sat down and waited, approached by a girl I knew from school whose dad offered me a ride home, but thinking Daddy and Mom would eventually show up, I turned down his offer. So, I continued to sit there, and as the clock ticked well past an hour, I finally gave up waiting and started walking toward home, which was approximately eight miles, give or take a mile, from Denton. Around three hours later, I finally reached Yawn Cemetery Road, and when I got to the house, no one was home but the dogs that ran to greet me, jumpin' and barkin' like they always did.

We always had farm dogs, a couple of which I remember: Jabbo, a birddog that had deformed feet that turned outward, and Boochie, a little fuzzy dog that was prone to running fits; he'd just take off running all over the place and in circles. One day, we were told to try mullein plant to cure him, so we got some, boiled it up, and gave it to him, and miraculously, he never had another running fit again.

With no one home, I petted the dogs and then decided to climb up in the chinaberry tree that stood in front of our house, where I hung around until the family returned. I was afraid Daddy might be mad at me for being sent home, and I hated disappointing him.

"What are you doing here?" Mom spotted me climbing down from the tree the moment they pulled up to the house, shooing the dogs away so they didn't jump on her. "How did you get home?"

She and Daddy had never gotten the note my aunt and uncle had sent stating that they were sending me home on the train, and Daddy, knowing that my whole experience had been a bad one, was sympathetic. I didn't make any money that week pickin' cotton, but I didn't care about the money, 'cause I was happy as a pig in mud to be back home with my family, where I belonged.

WAYCROSS WOES

1944

The year I turned eleven was an especially hard period of time for our family. Crops weren't bringing in enough money to survive on, forcing Daddy to leave Hazlehurst and seek work in other towns. We first moved to Waycross, where Daddy had found a job working as a section hand for the Atlantic Coast Line Railroad. It was hard work—laying rail ties and driving rail spikes—but Daddy did what he had to do for his family during those desperate times.

By then, Grandma Persons had passed away while staying with one of my mom's sisters, and the loss of her left me heartsick. I cried buckets of tears when she died, knowing I would miss her dearly. There was no finer or more loving a grandmother to be had.

Change was in the air, and life in Waycross called for a drastic adjustment from farm life to town life. While in Waycross, we lived in an old motel that had been converted into apartments, and Shirley and I attended Wacona School. Despite being eleven years old, I was only in the fourth grade due to failing two years of school, placing me behind other students my own age. I never thought life could get worse, but I was wrong, 'cause that was the year of the bully I will call Lionel.

Lionel was older than me. He was bigger than me. He was meaner than a mad rooster. He was a real bully. And every chance he got, he laid a whippin' on me, making my life miserable. Wacona School was about half a mile from our apartment, and I walked to and from school, a trek that allowed Lionel the opportunity he needed to catch me at the end of every school day. I would head straight for home as fast as I could run, keeping an ever-watchful eye out for him, but he usually caught me. He never let up. I was scared of him and dreaded facing him at school. He'd made it a mission to ruin my life, and I was sick of having bruises and black eyes, desperate for something to put an end to the abuse.

One Saturday, I spotted Lionel outside the place we were renting, and I ran inside and shut the door. No one else was home that day, and when Lionel found out that I was home alone, he came after me and pushed his way inside our apartment.

"Get out of my house, Lionel," I hollered at him, knowing he was fixin' to pound me.

I ran through the house and ended up in the kitchen, where, desperate to protect myself, I grabbed the first thing within reach, which just happened to be an ice pick. I gripped it tight in my fist, and then, in that moment of panic and without considering the consequences, I raised that ice pick and threw it, watching as it spun through the air in what seemed like slow motion.

"Ah!" Lionel hollered out when the ice pick lodged a good inch-deep in his knee.

I stood frozen as he yanked it out, certain that he was going to pound me, but instead of coming after me, he turned and hobbled away.

When he was out of the apartment, I slumped against the wall as the magnitude of what I'd done hit me. "I'm in real trouble now," I said aloud to myself.

I knew that once he'd tended to his knee, he'd want revenge, and I was right to have worried, 'cause that very next school day, he was worse than ever before. I needed help, so I decided to confide in an older cousin who was in his teens—someone who could handle a bully like Lionel.

"He's gonna kill me." I told my cousin about the ice pick toss. "It just made things worse."

"You should've told me sooner." He bumped my shoulder. "No one's gonna mess with my little cousin like that."

At the end of the next school day, I raced for home, and just as I had anticipated, Lionel was in hot pursuit. I ran hard and fast, praying he didn't catch me.

I glanced back, seeing he was gaining ground, watching as he punched his fist into his palm, getting warmed up to lay another whippin' on me.

"He's gonna kill me. He's gonna kill me," I mumbled over and again as I ran for dear life.

Suddenly, someone sprang out from behind some bushes. "Hey! Leave him alone!" a familiar voice yelled.

Looking back again, I'd never been so glad to see my cousin who was in hot pursuit of Lionel who was in hot pursuit of me, and knowing I had backup, I stopped running.

"Who are you?" Lionel faced my cousin.

"Someone who's here to make sure this is the last time you pick on Red." My cousin smacked his fist into his palm. "Let's see how you like it."

My cousin put a lickin' on Lionel that day, and my tormenter never picked on me again. In fact, shortly after that incident—the day of the bully whippin'—Lionel and I actually came to be pretty good friends. Who'd ever a thunk it?

School days were better for the rest of my time

at Wacona, but my challenges, while there, did not lay solely with Lionel, for I had another scuffle or two that year.

Mom, Daddy, Shirley, Ronald, and I had attended a Halloween party at the school one night, where I was caught off guard by another boy whom I will call Carl. He was dressed in a ridiculous clown costume, and for some unknown reason, charged at me upon approaching the door and shoved me down. I felt my cheek sting where my face struck the rocky ground, and losing my temper, I balled my hands into fists, ready to retaliate. I scrambled back onto my feet, eager to confront him, but he raced away before I could reciprocate, and I didn't see him again that night.

I fumed all evening, wondering why Carl had shoved me down in such a rotten way, thinking maybe it was because I hadn't worn a costume. Maybe he hated his own costume and had been made to wear it or ridiculed for it. Maybe it was a dare. Maybe.... Regardless of the many possible reasons, I wanted only one thing, and that was to even the score.

The next morning at school, when I spotted

Carl, I confronted him, and soon we were rollin' on the ground in an all-out tussle.

"Stop that, boys! Stop that fighting right now." Ms. Barbee broke up our scuffle.

"I'll get you back." I glared at Carl, ready to tear into him again.

Ms. Barbee sent the rest of the kids to class but kept me and Carl outside. "Follow me." She walked us to the front of the school and had us stand back to back. "If you have that much energy to fight, then you can do some running."

She instructed us to make laps around the school, running in opposite directions, and each time we passed each other, we were to stop and shake hands. So, I started running one way, and Carl the other, and when we met up on that first lap, I wanted nothing more than to punch his lights out, but uncertain if Ms. Barbee might be watching, I sucked in my bottom lip, held out my hand, and gave one quick shake.

I continued runnin', unable to expunge the mental image of rotten Carl shoving me down on that rocky ground, feeling my heart rate quicken and my face grow warm, partly from the exercise, but mostly from boiling anger.

"Another lap." Ms. Barbee waved me on as I approached her at the front of the school. "Keep running."

On that second lap, I stopped again when I met up with Carl and reluctantly shook his hand, still wanting to sock him a good one. By lap three, we were both getting worn out and slowing down, and I was beginning to care a little less about punching him in the mouth. By lap four, we were dripping with sweat and short of breath, and by lap five, my legs felt like rubber, and at that point, I just wanted Ms. Barbee's punishment to end, 'cause I couldn't take another lap.

"That's enough." Ms. Barbee finally stopped us. "I hope you've both learned your lesson."

"Yes ma'am." Carl and I answered through gasps.

"I'm glad to hear it. Now, shake hands again and make up," she told us.

I shook Carl's hand, not fully ready to make up, but for the sake of my tired legs and strained lungs, I pretended to put the conflict to rest.

After that shared experience, though, Carl and I never fought again, and we went on to become friends. I never did learn why he'd pushed me down that night at the Halloween party, but with the incident behind us, and with Ms. Barbee's lesson learned, it just didn't matter anymore.

Waycross presented many ups and downs, but I toughed it out, and along with the challenges of town life and school bullies, I even encountered a little suspense while living there. One night, I had just left our apartment, walking to a school function, when I spotted what appeared to be a person lying on the side of the road. It looked like a dead body, and my first thought was that someone had been hit by a car.

"Hey," I called out, imagining a bloody, messed-up corpse. "Are you okay?" My voice trembled as I inched closer, trying to determine if the dark, lumpy figure lying there was, in fact, a person. In the dark surroundings, it was hard to tell exactly what I was seeing.

My heart pounded as I drew closer, and I nearly

jumped out of my skin when the figure suddenly jerked and slid several feet in an unnatural manner. I yelled out and raced for the apartment, returning a few minutes later with Mom and Shirley, finding the figure still lying in the same spot. We, all three, carefully approached what we all agreed appeared to be a dead body, but when the figure moved again in that same creepy, unnatural fashion, Mom shrieked, and she, Shirley, and I all ran back to the apartment to get Daddy. He went back with us to investigate, but when we returned that last time, the body was gone.

The mystery of the dead body on the roadside remained unsolved until days later, when we discovered that several boys had been pranking folks with a dummy that they'd tied to a string and pulled to make it move and scare people who'd stopped to investigate. We'd been royally duped by those tricksters who, no doubt, had gotten a really good laugh at our expense. Boy oh boy, they'd certainly got us good, but as much as I hated being a target of pranksters, it was a relief to learn that there had never been a real person lying along the roadside that night.

The Red Hills of Home

After leaving Waycross and all of my Waycross woes behind me, we moved to Ocala, where Daddy agreed to help one of his brothers-in-law—a sister's husband—plant and harvest beans on his farm. Shirley and I attended school there, once again adjusting to new routines, people, and surroundings. When I wasn't in school, I was working in the fields, doing my part, just as I would have back in Handtown.

At that point, we had been away from Handtown for well over a year, but during our time away, my Uncle Hamp and his family had lived in our little shotgun house and upkept our farm. I remember being miserably homesick, just plain tired, wanting nothing more than to go home. That was something that didn't happen for a while longer, but after nearly two years away, we eventually headed back to Handtown, and I couldn't have been happier, 'cause there's simply no place like those red hills of home.

* * * *

AFTER RETURNING TO HAZLEHURST, I began

to enjoy going to school, and I started earning much better grades. I played on the basketball team at Brooker-Denton School, and I took pride in the sport. During games, the folks would often yell out to the coach to put Georgia Boy Red in the game. I was a good player, and I truly loved the sport.

Even though I was getting along better in school, I did, however, still get into a bit of trouble from time to time, palling around with Dubb, my partner in crime. He was nearly two years younger than me, but being in the same grade, we had become best friends.

One day at school, the class had been dismissed for lunch, but Dubb and I stayed behind in the classroom for an up-to-no-good motive—to see how hot we could get the classroom thermometer. It was one of those big teaching thermometers with a bulb at the bottom, and it hung on the wall, reaching from the floor to a height taller than I stood at that time.

"Let's see how hot we can get it," Dubb said, and he pulled out a box of oversized matches that we had with us.

We started lighting those matches and holding

the flames under that bulb, watching as the red liquid rose higher and higher and higher, until...kaboom! The thermometer exploded, splattering red-dyed alcohol everywhere, and before we thought to run, our teacher came rushing in, catching us, literally, red-handed.

"What are you doing in here?" she yelled. "Look at the mess you've made."

I knew right where we were headed, straight to the principal's office to face that paddle full of holes that he'd used on me once or twice before. I was well aware of its sting.

"He's gonna whip us good," I told Dubb as we sat and awaited judgment.

We then spotted some magazines and got a brilliant idea to shove them in the seat of our pants to cushion the blows of that dreaded holey paddle. So, jumping into action, we did just that, and when we were called in to receive our paddlin', that ol' principal tore up those magazines that lined our pants, never knowing we'd padded our britches, sparing our tushies a terrible burn.

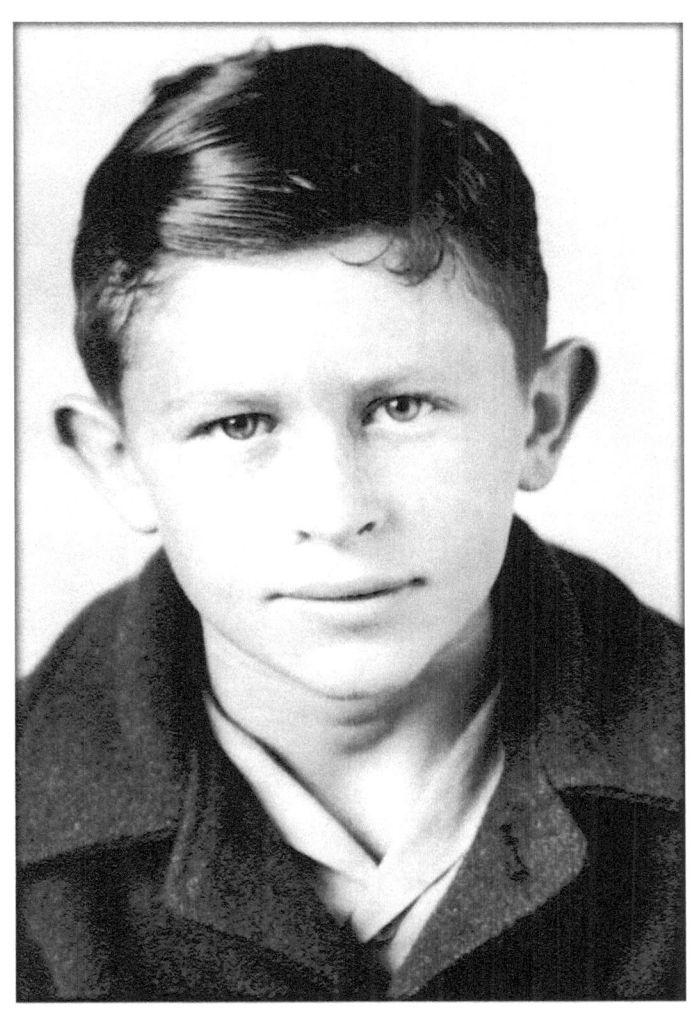

EARLY TEEN YEARS

In 1946, I had reached my early teen years. My little, dark-haired sister, Shirley, was ten, and my brother, Ronald, was then six years old. Shirley, like most little sisters, followed me around a lot, and I'd get irritated with her. One evening, while milking Irene, an auburn-colored cow we'd raised—I often milked them morning and night—Shirley was spying through the stall boards at me, thinking I didn't know she was there. So, to teach her a lesson, I pointed one of the Jersey's teats at her and squirted her in the face. She hollered at me and ran for the house, calling: Mama, Mama,

Mama, tattling what I'd done. Mom would scold me for pickin' on my sister, but I couldn't resist the occasional tomfoolery. Little pranks, like a squirt of milk in the face, that's all it took to get her dander up.

Milking our cows was usually a painless chore, thanks to Daddy's training sessions. He'd teach them by leading 'em into a narrow stall for milking, where they didn't have much room to move around, and he'd give them some feed to keep 'em busy while he acclimated them to the process. Usually, all went relatively well, but if one got rowdy and kicked him too hard, Daddy was known to kick 'em back.

After training, the cows might still get a little testy from time to time, but all in all, they were typically well-behaved. We did, however, have a young cow once that presented Daddy with a real challenge on one occasion. She had just calved her first baby and wouldn't allow her calf to nurse, so we bottle-fed the baby, hoping that the mother would eventually nurse him. Soon, Daddy realized that the mother cow's utter was enormously engorged, and to prevent problems or infection, he needed to relieve her of her excess milk. Getting to the task, he got a bucket and reached down to pull her teats, and that cow kicked at him and ran off, her swollen utter so inflated that it looked like it might pop at any given moment. I laughed at the hilarious sight of Daddy chasing that big-uttered milk cow, trying several more times to milk her, only to get kicked with every attempt.

Getting fed up, Daddy finally took that ol' cow into a stall and tried to milk her there, but she still wasn't havin' it. At his wits' end, Daddy then tied her front legs to one post and her back legs to another, and during all of the wrestling going on inside that enclosure, that ornery cow somehow ended up tipped over and rolled onto her back, with Daddy sitting on top of her, milking her in topsy-turvy fashion, upside down, once and for all.

When he was done, that young cow got up with no further issues, and believe it or not, started letting her baby nurse. She must have either felt better after being milked or decided, after that ordeal, that she'd rather let the baby nurse than be milked again by Daddy. Anyway, we never had any more trouble out of her, and both mama and baby were fine after that event.

As a rule, we milked our cows twice every day and filled jugs that we'd lower into the well to keep cold, always having three or four jugs on hand that we could pull up whenever we needed milk for cooking or simply for a cold drink. Mom would also leave milk out for several days to make cream and butter. We had a plunge churn that she'd stand over and work a staff up and down, until butter formed. It was a lengthy process, but in the end, well worth the effort, 'cause there was nothing else like the taste of country butter.

I spent a lot of time in our old crib barn. During the winter, I used to sit up in the hayloft and pick peanuts out of the hay and eat them. We stored a lot of peanut hay that we grew and harvested as food for our livestock. We also grew millet. I remember taking a scythe and heading out into the field, where I'd start swingin', gathering cut grass into bundles to dry before hauling to the barn. We got hay from several sources, including gathering shocks of fodder leaves from the corn field. We'd tie them using one of the long cornstalk leaves, and either wedge the bunches between tight sections of cornstalks or hang 'em from ears of corn until dry and ready to later collect. We were pretty self-sufficient with what we had, but we did buy extra feed and hay whenever possible.

We continued to attend church on a regular basis, dressing up in our Sunday best—Mom and Shirley wearing their prettiest dresses, and us boys sporting our best shirts and trousers. I always cleaned up well, despite my trouser length tending to consistently rise a bit short due to growing so fast. That, along with an issue of holey shoes—not of the anointed kind, but as in worn out—were typical issues to contend with at that age, and it didn't bother me in the least.

The church periodically had baptism services at a nearby body of water called the Baptism Hole. It lay southeast of the church, next to Hurrikin (Hurricane Creek), just a hop, skip, and a jump away. Kids in the community often went there to swim, and I should mention that I almost drowned there on one occasion. I was down there swimming with one of my older cousins D.L. and a friend of his whom I'll call Albert, and we were roughhousing a bit. Being so much younger, I would climb up on their shoulders, stand up, and dive into the water; but upon making one last dive that day into an area of deep water, I suddenly found myself choking and unable to breathe. D.L. and Albert were wading toward the bank to head home when I surfaced from my dive, and they didn't immediately notice that I was in distress. Luckily, they looked back and saw that I was in trouble and hurried back into the water to help me. They carried me to the bank, slapped my back and pumped my stomach until I was free of the water that was choking me, allowing me to finally breathe again.

That was the day I nearly drowned at the Baptism Hole, but that experience didn't stop me from goin' back there swimming time and again, and around the age of thirteen, I was baptized in that very same body of water during one of our church baptism services.

On my day of baptism, the congregation drove over to the water hole, some by horse and wagon, others in their cars, and gathered along the bank. How fitting the occasion were the hymns "Nothing But the Blood" and "Are You Washed in the Blood?" On that day of baptism, I recall stepping into a line of more than 20 participants that included my cousin Judon and our good friend Edmund to await my turn to wade out into waist-deep water and be baptized by the preacher. However, my main memory of that event is not so much of my own baptism, but that of a girl who got baptized along with the rest of us that day. She was a little older than me, tall and thin, an athletic girl who was on the basketball team at school—a star player. She seemed so outgoing and confident that I was surprised to learn that she struggled with an unfortunate fear of being dunked underwater.

We inched along, making our way deeper into the water, and when her time came to step up to the young preacher for her moment of baptism, she froze, nervously gnawing on her bottom lip.

"It's your turn." Pastor Ledford took her hand and guided her in front of him. "Do you believe that Jesus is the Son of God and that He died on the cross and rose from the dead for the forgiveness of your sins? Do you accept Him as your Lord and Savior?"

Still gnawing on her bottom lip, she answered yes in a shaky voice.

"I baptize you in the name of the Father, Son, and Holy Spirit." Pastor Ledford said his blessing, had her pinch her nose, and attempted to dip her backward, but to his surprise, she suddenly twisted away from him and nearly pushed him over.

"I'm so sorry." She was embarrassed, hearing the congregation erupt in laughter. "I'm afraid to be dunked underwater."

"It's okay." Pastor Ledford wiped his face that was splashed with water. "Let's give it another try."

He endeavored to baptize her again, but just like his first failed attempt, she twisted and nearly pushed him over a second time. Pastor Ledford was determined to see her baptized, though, and with a third attempt, he decided to give the undertaking a little more effort to finally get the job done. So, once more, the preacher attempted to dip her backward, this time with added momentum, but in an unexpected turn off events, she grabbed ahold of his shoulders and initiated a rollover maneuver that no one saw coming and dunked him underwater in her place. Almost instantly, Pastor Ledford sprang up from the dunk, momentarily stunned, met by a roar of laughter from the congregation.

"Hey, preacher, I bet *you* didn't count on gettin' baptized today," one brethren called out, bringing about another wave of laughter.

It took some time, but Pastor Ledford refused to give up and finally got the girl baptized. "Your name will be written in the book of life," he told her, all dripping wet, as the congregation clapped their hands and rejoiced.

Pastor Ledford then moved on with baptizing the rest of us, for he still had quite a few people in line awaiting their turn. "Step on over, Red." He motioned for me.

I waded out to him, and said, "Don't worry, preacher, I ain't afraid of the water."

I knew the excitement of my baptism would pale in comparison to the colorful event I'd just witnessed, and it was over in two shakes of a lamb's tail. I was happy to be officially baptized, though, and to this day, I've never felt cleaner than that day I rose up from the muddy waters of the Baptism Hole, washed in the blood of the lamb.

Romans 10:9

"That if thou shalt confess with thy mouth the Lord Jesus, and shalt believe in thine heart that God hath raised him from the dead, thou shalt be saved."

* * * *

OL' MAUDE WASN'T A VERY PRETTY HORSE, an old gray swayback, big-bellied and a little mulish. She was Granddad's horse, and Judon—he lived about a quarter mile west of Granddad's farm—and I would meet up and ride ol' Maude bareback in the big pine woods.

One day, we were out there ridin' (Judon in front and me in back) when he said: "Let's run this ol' horse back to the house, Red."

I said, "Alright. Get 'er a goin'."

He gave ol' Maude a tap with his heels and she took off in a fast trot that quickened into a gallop, running hard for home. We were laughing and holding on tight, when that ol' horse suddenly took a sharp turn and threw us off. I, luckily, only knocked my hand against a small limb, but poor Judon landed chest-first against one of those big, towering pines and slid down its rough bark, skinning his belly raw.

I jumped up from the ground and tried to catch Maude, but she kept running and left us to walk all the way home, where we found her waitin' at her pen. I took off her bridle, and she happily trotted off like nothin' ever happened, but Judon wasn't nearly as spry, in desperate need of some patching up.

Riding ol' Maude down in the big pine woods. Those were fun times that we had again and again after that sharp-turn-Maude-maneuver incident, and we always laughed when we rode by Judon's special tree.

Around that time, I was wanting a horse of my own, and Daddy surprised me by buying me one from a man in Douglas. It was a small horse, not exactly a pony, but also not more than 14 hands tall. The day we got him home, I was eager to ride him, and I immediately saddled him up. I climbed on and gave him a light tap on the side, gripping that saddle horn for dear life when he bolted and tore off across the field in an all-out gallop.

"Woah!" I shouted and pulled back on the reins, to no avail.

That little horse—Billy—had that bit clenched tight in his teeth, and there was no stopping him as he headed straight for the fence, where he threw me off.

Mom, who was running with Daddy across the field after me and Billy, was afraid I was hurt, but I didn't have a scratch.

"He just needs a little more trainin'." Daddy helped me up and brushed me off. "The more you ride him, the better he'll get."

Daddy was right, 'cause in a couple of weeks Billy was minding great, and I loved riding him. I'd often ride him over to Judon's house, and one day, while heading there, I came upon another rider at the crossroads. It was my friend Dubb's dad, John, and he was riding his big ol' horse that made little Billy look itsy-bitsy in comparison.

"How about a race, Red," John challenged.

"No. There's no way my tiny horse can keep up

with yours."

"Oh, come on, let's see how fast he can run," he kept after me until I agreed.

So, we raced the horses in the direction of my Uncle Marcus's place—Judon's house—with Billy shooting off like a bullet, leaving John and his big ol' horse in the dust. After a short distance, I stopped and waited for John to catch up.

"I can't believe it. I just can't believe it," he kept saying. "That little ol' horse sure can run."

After that day, I would often meet up with Dubb who rode his dad's big horse, but I never had to worry about being challenged to a race again, seein' as he knew the outcome of the race I'd had with John. Needless to say, I was proud of my little horse, Billy. He may have been small in size, but he was large in stature.

THANKFUL FOR DADDY

Chicken for supper was a frequent meal, and Daddy would chew up those chicken bones and suck the marrow right out of 'em. He had strong, solid teeth. In all his days, he'd never been to a dentist, and amazingly, he'd never had a bad tooth or a toothache. My theory is that the minerals and calcium from all that marrow kept his teeth strong. It certainly wasn't from drinking milk, 'cause Daddy didn't like milk and never drank it; but he was fortunate to have had the strong teeth he was blessed with, seein' as he enjoyed playing a juice harp that he'd bite between his teeth while plucking folksy tunes. Not being a musical talent like Mom, he didn't play any instruments, but he enjoyed playin' that juice harp now and again, and I loved hearin' it.

Daddy was a kind, patient, and hard-working man. He hardly ever lost his temper; a good-natured, easy-going individual. He wasn't a man who enjoyed disciplining his kids, having only whipped me once in my life, and with ample justification, for I fully deserved it. I'll never forget the day it happened, he and I were down in the field late one morning with our mule, Emer, and a wagon stacked full of fertilizer, trying to put it out before any chance of rain hindered the job. With Emer hitched to the fertilizer spreader, we filled the hopper and moved fast, as it looked like a storm might be gathering. We were working hard when Uncle Clifton—Winnette's dad—and Tilmon, one of his sons, came walking toward us.

"Hey there." Uncle Clifton called over to us. "We're headed down to the Big Lake to do some fishin'. You wanna come along?"

I quickly answered, "Yeah. I believe I will."

"Not today, son," Daddy quickly chimed in. "We've got to get this fertilizer out," he told Uncle Clifton.

"Well, maybe next time." Uncle Clifton and Tilmon went on their way.

"I want to go fishin' with them, Daddy," I whined.

"Not today. We have too much work."

Disregarding what he said, I laid everything down and started walking away, brushing off the front of my worn overalls that were coated in red dust that matched my carrottop.

"Where do you think you're goin'?" Daddy hollered at me.

"I'm going fishin' with Uncle Clifton and Tilmon."

"No, you're not. I told you, we've got to get this fertilizer out." He walked toward a nearby persimmon tree.

I argued, "They're going down to the Big Lake. I want to catch some fish."

"Get back here, right now." Daddy ordered with

authority while cutting a branch off the tree.

I ignored him and kept walking away, eager to catch up with Uncle Clifton and Tilmon, when a moment later, I felt Daddy's hand grip my arm. I then felt something sting the back of my legs and realized he was whippin' me with that persimmon tree branch he'd just cut off the tree.

"I, told, you, son, you, are, not, goin'," he made clear between each swat.

I danced about, feeling the burn of the branch on the back of my legs, shocked that Daddy was doing such a thing.

"Now," he stopped after those eight swats, "like I said, get back to that fertilizer," he ordered.

Without argument or delay, I hurried back to work, putting out fertilizer as hard and as fast as I could, like there was no tomorrow. I cried as I worked, not because of my stinging legs, but from hurt feelings.

When we finally finished spreading fertilizer around 3 o'clock, Daddy headed toward the back of the field. "Come on," he called to me. "Bring Emer, and we'll tie her to the back fence."

"Where are we going?" I didn't know what he was doing. "Home's the other way."

"We're going fishin'." He motioned for me to come along. "Let's go."

I ran to catch up with him, and we hopped over the hog wire fence and headed for Hurrikin.

"Daddy, we don't have any hooks, line, poles, or bait."

"Don't worry. We'll get some fish," he assured me.

When we got to the creek, he zeroed in on a particular spot and told me to jump in the water. He followed me in and led me to a log lying on the creek bottom. We dove down and pulled that old log out of the water—he had one end and I had the other—and we carried it over to the bank, tilted it up, and poured two catfish out of its hollowed-out center.

"Let's get some more." Daddy headed back into the water.

He knew where all of those old hollow logs were, and we dove down a couple more times, pulling them up and pouring out those fish. When we had more than enough to fry for dinner, we tossed those hollow logs back in the creek, gathered up our catfish, and headed for home. We talked as we went, and Daddy was sorry for whippin' me with the persimmon branch. I was sorry, too, for defying his authority and not minding him in front of Uncle Clifton and Tilmon, who no doubt overheard some of our earlier embarrassing exchange.

That was the day I got my one and only whippin' Daddy ever gave me. It was also the best day I ever had fishin' for catfish with him, not that we didn't have other great times fishin' together, 'cause we did, many times, but because of the sentiment behind the reason for going to the lake that afternoon. It was his way of making amends for those eight swats, and it did, for after that day our bond was all the more meaningful and strong. I was always so thankful for Daddy.

* * * *

DADDY APPRECIATED A GOOD JOKE, and I loved to prank him every so often. One cold winter night, a front had just settled over our area, causing temperatures to plummet into the upper twenties. Without finished walls, our house was freezing cold, so we decided to go to bed early that evening and bundled up under heavy covers in an effort to keep warm.

Earlier that afternoon, before supper, I'd gotten the bright idea to take a Coca Cola bottle and fill it with water. I plugged it with a fishing cork, tapped a little nail into the end, and attached a string to the head of the nail. I then sneaked into Mom and Daddy's room, went to Daddy's bed, hid the bottle way down under his covers, and tied the string to the footboard. Lying in my own bed that night, I could faintly hear Mom and Daddy talking in their room, patiently waiting for Daddy to find the bottle, which he eventually did.

"Nellie, somethin's in my bed," he said.

Knowing that was the moment I'd been waitin' for, I got out of bed and eased toward their room. The house was freezing, but I didn't want to miss his reaction.

"Ah!" Daddy suddenly hollered.

"What's wrong?" Mom said with alarm.

"I'm all wet!"

I saw light beneath their door and knew he'd lit a lantern.

"It's a bottle," he mumbled, "with a string tied to the footboard...Red!"

I heard his feet striking the planked floor and knew he was coming after me.

"Red!" He stormed out of the room in his bare feet. "It's too cold for this nonsense."

I laughed and ran, thinking he wouldn't pursue me in his bare feet, but I was wrong. Ronald and Shirley stumbled out of bed to a ruckus of Daddy chasing me all over the house, till he couldn't take the cold anymore and had to get out of his wet clothes.

In retrospect, I probably could have chosen a better night for shenanigans, especially a water prank that soaked him and his bed, but it was all done in good-humored fun.

* * * *

WHEN I WAS YOUNG, I sometimes walked in my

sleep. Daddy said I usually just wandered around the house, having found me one night curled up on the supper table with no idea how I'd gotten there. My brother also walked in his sleep once, only he wandered a little farther than the supper table.

It was a dark night, well past midnight, when Daddy woke me up asking where my brother was, 'cause he wasn't in bed. Ronald and I shared a room, but having been asleep, I had no idea where he'd gone.

"Get up. We need to look for him." Daddy set down a lantern he was carryin' and lit a second one. "I've already checked the house." He handed me one of the lanterns. "We need to search outside."

I could tell that Daddy was mighty worried as I scrambled out of bed, slipped on my shoes, and followed him to the back door of the house. Upon stepping outside, I suddenly paused on the porch when I heard a familiar laugh...Ronald's laugh. "I hear him," I told Daddy.

"Where is he?" Daddy followed the sound of Ronald's laughter that led us toward the crib barn.

"There he is." I spotted my brother perched

high up on the slatted wood fence that enclosed Billy and Emer.

"What are you doing out here, son?" Daddy called out to him.

Ronald didn't answer.

"I think he's sleepwalkin', Daddy."

Ronald's eyes were wide open, and he appeared to be awake, but he didn't respond to us. He teetered on the top rail of that locked fence, laughing and cheering at something in dreamland, utterly confusing poor ol' Emer and Billy.

"Hold this." Daddy handed me his lantern, climbed up on the fence, and woke Ronald up.

"What am I doing out here?" Ronald mumbled in confusion as Daddy helped him down.

"Sleepwalkin'." Daddy laughed and steered him toward the back porch.

With everyone back inside the house, safe and sound, we all settled down again for the night. I crawled into bed, ready to enter my own dreamland, glancing over at Ronald who had already fallen back asleep. Lying there, I stared up at the rafters reviewing the

DILAPIDATED CRIB BARN.

events of the night as I drifted off to sleep, relieved that everything had turned out fine, so very thankful for Daddy who was always our protector.

BAD CHOICES

My Aunt Artha was quite a self-reliant lady, and I enjoyed spending time with her. She'd often ask me to go fishin' with her, and many times, before heading out to the lake, she'd send me to do some worm fiddling for bait. I'd hammer a stob into the ground and rub it with a brick, making vibrations that lured those worms right up from the earth.

Aunt Artha also did a lot of fishin' on her own. She certainly knew how to catch catfish. She'd go down to the Big Lake before dark and set out poles along the bank, then she'd go back at daybreak to claim her catch.

Early one morning, a cousin and I headed down to the lake to do some fishin' and check some lines we had set out the day before, and when we got there, we came upon several poles actively bobbin'. Only they weren't our poles.

"Look at that," my cousin said. "Aunt Artha hasn't been here yet to check her poles, and she's got a fish on every one of 'em."

The tips of her cane poles were just a jumpin', a pleasing sight for any fisherman returning to check their lines.

"Let's get some of her catfish, Red." He pulled in one of the poles that had hooked a big one. "Aunt Artha will never know we took a couple."

"Well," I quickly scanned our surrounding, "okay." I, too, was overcome by temptation and helped pull in two more of her lines, stealing three of her fish in total.

We then set her lines back out and moved on to our own trotlines at the other end of the lake, all the while, keeping a watchful eye out for Aunt Artha.

"There she is." My cousin soon spotted her. "Good thing she didn't show up ten minutes earlier. She'd have caught us."

We watched as she checked her poles, and I moaned with pangs of guilt. "I feel terrible for taking her catfish. She's gonna know we took 'em. The ground's all wet over there from us pulling 'em in."

Several minutes later, after she'd checked her lines, she tossed us a wave and came over to talk. "You boys sure are out here early." She looked at the fish we had. "I see y'all caught some catfish."

"Yeah. We got a few on the hooks we set out," we told her.

She didn't say anything for an awkward moment, and I knew that she knew what we'd done—stolen her catfish off her poles.

"I didn't get many this morning." She held up two fish, then looked me directly in the eyes with an accusing stare, a look that I interpreted as "Shame on you, Red".

"Well, enjoy those fish, boys. I'll be sure to get out here a little earlier tomorrow."

As she headed away, I felt my body slump, weighted down by shame and remorse over the bad choice we'd made. "We shouldn't have taken her catfish." I was angry with myself 'cause I loved Aunt Artha. "We shouldn't have done it."

That was one bad choice I always regretted, attributing our actions to simply being young and thoughtless. I understand, today, that areas of the human brain that control decision-making don't fully develop until early adulthood, and immature, we certainly were. I try not to fully hobble on that crutch, though, 'cause I was raised right and taught good values. All I can say is: Oh, the questionable things we often do in our youth; the downright rotten things at times. I just hope Aunt Artha knew my true regrets and forgave me and my cousin for our immaturity, insensitivity, and utter stupidity, 'cause afterwards, we indeed felt like pond scum for stealin' her catfish.

Psalm 69:5

"O God, thou knowest my foolishness; and my sins are not hid from thee."

BAD CHOICES

* * * *

ONE DAY, WHILE PLOWING down in the field, Mom hollered for me to come to dinner. I was working near one of our terraces—we had two about 500' apart to prevent runoff—when I heard her call, and having more plowing to do that afternoon, I led our mule, Emer, over to the shade of the chinaberry tree that canopied our front yard, intending to tie her off to the fence while I went inside to eat. I looped the rope through the hog wire and was just about to yank it tight, when a chicken suddenly flew down from an overhanging limb and soared right over Emer's head, sending her rearing from sudden fright.

In that instant, a sharp pain shot through my hand, and I expelled a yell that drew Mom to our front porch. In the blink of an eye, the tip of my right ring finger had nearly been severed, having been caught between the rope and fence when Emer reared up. I held out my hand and the tip of my finger dangled by a mere sliver of flesh.

"My finger!" I gripped my hand and ran toward

the house, meeting Mom in the doorway.

"What happened?" She saw that my hand was bleeding and ushered me inside.

Daddy hurried over and said, "Uh-oh, that's not good," when he saw the tip of my finger nearly torn off and laying on the back of my hand. "We better take you to see the doctor." He headed outside to put Emer away and met us at the car.

Minutes later, we were en route to Hazlehurst, where I soon found myself sitting in an examination room, face to face with a medical professional.

"We'll just make a clean cut at the joint." The doctor examining my injury was about to remove the whole tip of my finger when another doctor intervened and stopped him.

As luck would have it, a specialist from Atlanta happened to be in the office that day.

"No. Don't you cut that boy's finger off," the specialist said. "Sew that severed portion right back on. It'll reattach and heal."

I thought for sure that I was going to lose the tip of my finger that day, but thanks to the specialist from

Atlanta, it was saved. They sewed it back on, and just as he'd stated, it reattached. It was never perfect, healing somewhat misshapen, mostly due to the fact that I'd played a school basketball game that week instead of giving it the proper time to heal. Boy oh boy, it sure was sore that next day, and I knew I'd messed up. It continued to heal, though, and at least I still had my full finger, unlike my mom who'd lost a pinkie finger when she was a girl—cut off by her brother.

That was a story I'd heard many times. Her brother thought she'd pull her hand away from the chopping block, and she never thought he'd actually chop her hand. It was a dare gone wrong that had left her with a stub tinged blue from ash used to stop the bleeding. Yet, the loss of her pinkie had never stopped her from doing the things she'd loved, including playing piano and her mandolin. I imagine, however, that my incident probably carried her back to that trauma she'd suffered of losing her own pinkie finger to the blade of a hatchet. Oh, the bad choices we often unfortunately make, and the crazy things kids do.

* * * *

ONE OF MY COUSINS, Comer, who was a younger brother of Winnette and Tilmon—they had several more siblings—would meet up with me on hot summer days to go swimming in a pond near their house on Taylor Road. One fine day, Comer and I had just left the pond and decided to stop and visit one of his older brothers, who offered us some beer to cool us off. Although we were too young to drink alcohol, we took it, and the more beer he fed us, the longer we visited.

By the time afternoon had transitioned to evening, we had consumed so much beer that we were downright drunk, and what had started out as fun and games suddenly wasn't so much fun anymore. I grew extremely thirsty, and the more beer I drank, the thirstier I got. Dizziness followed, then nausea, and knowing I was in bad shape, I delayed going home, hoping to sober up before facing Mom and Daddy. As the hour grew late, I eventually had to leave, though, and reluctantly headed for home, stumbling along the trail that led through the pine woods between Taylor Road and our farm on Yawn Cemetery. Still dizzy and throwing up, I was plagued by a splitting headache that pounded like a bass drum, walking what felt like the longest trek of my life. Finally reaching home, I tried to slip inside the house without being seen, but Mom, with her keen intuition, was watching and waiting, and she immediately zeroed in on me.

"What's wrong with you?" She stepped close. "Your face and eyes are all red."

"I'm sick," I told her.

"What's the matter with you?" She kept after me.

"I was swimming all day. I think I spent too much time in the water." I could tell she was suspicious.

"You don't look right. Is that all you've been up to?"

Mom knew me too well to fool her.

"I—" Before I got another word out, I rushed back out the door, heaving over the edge of the porch, sicker than I'd ever been.

A minute later, I stumbled back inside and confessed that I'd been drinking beer all day and was sick from overdrinking. She scolded me a little and sent me to bed, and I stayed sick as a dog all night long.

I think back on some of the bad choices I made as a boy, and this incident ranks mighty close to the top of my list of stupid things I'd done in my youth. My first time drinking beer. Suffice it to say, it was not a good experience, and I never cared for the taste of beer after that miserable night.

Proverbs 23:32

"At the last it biteth like a serpent, and stingeth like an adder."

TOBACCO CROPS & TURPENTINE TREES

After completing my ninth grade in school, I had to place my education on the back burner and quit school to work full time on the farm. I also lent a hand to my uncles and cousins whenever they needed it, whether that be helping with their crops, clearing stumps with dynamite, or any other jobs needin' to be done. I had a lot to keep me busy at home, though, always out in the fields, working our crops. When plowing, I'd gee and haw the whole day, and Emer knew her commands. We couldn't have had a better mule. She pulled wagons. She dragged logs. She pulled tobacco sleds. We even used her when digging a pond on our land, a time-consuming job that was done by scooping out loads of dirt with a drag bucket pulled by Emer. She did it all, but being the mule of a crop farmer, her main job was to pull the wagon and plow.

We grew a lot of tobacco as our cash crop, but we also grew corn and cotton. All three brought in money, but while tobacco was an important crop for income, corn was a necessity for survival. That's one thing we always had—corn. I remember going with Daddy to take loads of it to a grit mill in Denton to have it ground, and they'd always keep some for payment. That's how we got our grits, which we ate practically daily.

Our crops were our livelihood, and working those red clay fields was hard work, having no means of hiring help; however, when the time came to harvest our crops, family and friends would rally together and get the jobs done. On those days of harvest, we'd cook up a big dinner for everyone who'd come to help.

Daddy, being one of twelve children, never had a lot of wealth in life, but he was rich in family. We had a large, extended circle of relatives living in and around Hazlehurst, and in those challenging times, it was a comfort to know that we had each other to rely on. Daddy was born in 1909 and farming was the only way of life he knew. I remember him talking about hardships farmers had faced when he was a boy, recalling the boll weevil infestations that decimated cotton crops in Georgia from the time he was around the age of six, plaguing cotton crops for years thereafter. He recalled severe droughts that occurred during the 1920s and how life was a struggle even prior to the Great Depression that struck the country in 1929, reaching its lowest point the year I was born, in 1933. Farming was an unpredictable way of life. It took a whole lot of prayer, faith, and trust in God.

Harvesting tobacco in late summer was a miserable, drawn-out endeavor, as the days were long and hot. As harvest neared, the plants were topped by hand, removing the buds and killing any hornworms that were eating the leaves. Soon, we were pickin' the first yellowing bottom leaves, gathering bundles under our arms, and filling sleds pulled by our mule, Emer. It was sticky, tiring labor, working our way a little higher up the plants each week, over a period of approximately 5 weeks.

We'd rise at daybreak and work those long rows, priming those ripening bottom yellowing leaves, then haul each load to the tobacco barn. There, in the shade of a shed roof that was attached to the side of the barn and covered a bench, we'd string those leaves onto long sticks before hanging them inside the barn from overhead, horizontal tier poles. It was a process we'd continue until the multi-level rooms (the vertical space in between the tier poles) in the barn were full and ready for flue-curing by means of a wood furnace that smoldered over the course of a week. Large pipes running through the barn would carry heat and smoke from the fire, the hot pipes radiating heat that dried out the tobacco leaves, until they were crisp and ready for market. The curing stage was critical, and we took turns sleeping on the bench under the shed roof at night, keeping a close eye on the fire, making sure to keep it stoked and burning.

Tobacco farming was an exhausting

RENOVATED TOBACCO BARN FROM MY CHILDHOOD HOMESTEAD.

undertaking, but it was a reliable crop. Emer and I spent hours on end out in our fields plowing, planting, fertilizing, hoeing and weedin' the many rows of whatever crops we were growing. We were out there no matter the heat or cold, no matter the aches and pains, 'cause that was the life of a farmer.

* * * *

A LOT OF OLD-GROWTH PINES stood on our 86 acres of land, and for extra income, Daddy used to tap them for resin using the cup and gutter method—what we referred to as workin' the turpentine trees. We'd chip an area of bark and streak the tree with an angled slash to get the pine sap oozing. Below that, we'd notch the tree and insert a gutter (a thin galvanized iron strip around two inches wide and a few inches long) to direct the gum into a rectangular cup affixed to the tree beneath the gutter by means of a nail.

Tapping trees took time, and as each gash stopped producing sap, new streaks would be scored directly above the preceding ones, slowly working

CATFACE ON THE REMAINS OF AN OLD PINE TREE IN HANDTOWN.

vertically up the sides of the trees with angled, parallel cuts that eventually reached upwards of six feet in height. Over time, the scars left by those streaks formed a distinct pattern that resembled the whiskers of a cat, lending to the term later attached to them as catface trees.

I spent many a day workin' the turpentine trees, and when the cups were full and ready for dipping, we'd carry buckets and collect the sap to fill 60-gallon wooden barrels hauled on the back of a wagon and pulled by our mule from tree to tree. Then, when we had full barrels—we were pretty much a two-barrel farm, but sometimes had more—we'd load 'em onto a truck and haul 'em down to a turpentine still in Nicholls, where we sold our supply. It was a long and sticky process, leaving those old trees scarred with catfaces, but in those days, tapping for resin brought in extra income, and every little bit helped.

I remember being hot and tired after a hard day of workin' those turpentine trees, and Daddy would say, "Let's go to the spring and cool off."

We would head toward Uncle Thomas's

property, to where a natural spring bubbled up from the ground, the cool and crystal-clear water a blessing to a parched tongue and overheated body. A long-stemmed drinking gourd always hung on the curb, and we'd dip that water and pour it over our head and shoulders, thankful for the instant relief those magical waters brought to us.

Workin' turpentine trees was a reliable fallback that got us through many cash-strapped times, including holiday seasons. Just before Christmas, Mom would send us out to scrape what sap we could for Christmas money. We counted on that income. Everyone in the area worked those trees for extra money, including my Uncle Clifton, who I'd sometimes help when he'd go out to tap them. I remember how he used to sing while he worked, his primary tune being the folk song "Froggy Went a-Courtin'". Sometimes, while out in the woods, I'd hear that tune drifting through the big pines, knowing that it was Uncle Clifton singin' while he worked those turpentine trees.

"Froggy went a-courtin' and he did ride, uh-huh...."

HANDTOWN HAUNTS

The Philadelphia Quartet, that's what we called ourselves. We were a singing group of four boys—me, along with Edmund and two of my cousins, Judon and Tilmon. My sister, Shirley, helped us out by playing the piano, and we grew to be pretty good, eventually receiving invitations to sing at churches and a few other places around town, including driving over to Douglas on several occasions to sing on the radio for a preacher's broadcast program.

In 1950, southern gospel quartet groups, such as the Blackwood Brothers, had grown popular since the

Depression days, and that's the style of music we sang, with Edmund singin' lead, Tilmon singin' tenor, Judon singin' baritone, and me singin' bass. We'd cover songs like "I'll Fly Away" and "Just a Closer Walk with Thee". With piano accompaniment, or a cappella, we sounded great and had a flair for performing.

We'd often practice at Edmunds house, over on what is now the junction of Greg Wilcox Rd and Theo Wilcox Cir, the latter of which was a shortcut that passed next to the church and cemetery. One night, after practicing pretty late, I had to walk home alone, as Shirley wasn't with me that evening, and it was over a mile to my house. The night was still and quiet, too quiet, as I started along the shortcut that circled by the church, unnerved by the eerie calm, aware of every shadowy movement in the surrounding darkness. The wind picked up as I neared the church cemetery. I felt my stomach knot. I did not want to pass the cemetery. I glanced out at the distant headstones glowing in the hazy moonlight, and I shuddered inside. A chill swept up my spine, and I slowed to a standstill, eyes wide, frozen in the grasp of a hair-raising sight of the headstones swayin' to and fro in dreamlike horror. Then, as I stood there, I thought I saw figures aimlessly wandering through the graveyard. Ghosts!

"Lord have mercy." My heart pounded fast and hard. "Run," I told myself, feeling my heart rate drum faster and faster. "Run." I forced my body to move.

My feet then picked up pace, and soon I was in an all-out run, heading for Yawn Cemetery Road and home as fast as my legs would carry me.

To this day, I'm not sure why that cemetery appeared so haunting to me that night. Obviously, my mind had been playing tricks on me, but after that event, I never walked past those graves again while alone at night. When practicing at Edmunds, I made sure I headed home before dark, never forgetting that eerie moonlit night, those swayin' headstones, and the overwhelming fear of what I'd imagined to be the ghosts of Handtown.

* * * *

DOWN ON HURRIKIN ONE NIGHT, Ronald and

I were out there fishin' when the strangest sounds arose in the nearby swampy woods.

"What in tarnation is that?" Ronald stopped and listened. "Sounds like people out here havin' a ball."

Jumbled whoops, hollers, and shrieks drifted from our dark surroundings, along with the moan of a breeze pushing through the towering pines, filling me with a sense of unease. I stood puzzled, thinking that those mysterious noises emanating from the unseen depths of those woods didn't exactly sound human, and all sorts of notions started running through my mind. Why would people be out here so late at night? I saw no lights in sight, only pitch darkness. Then, an unnerving thought popped into my mind—bigfoot—and that brought to mind a time years before, when Daddy and Granddad went out hunting one evening and took me, Mom, and Shirley along for the ride. We had stopped at the side of the swamp, and Daddy and Granddad headed toward the creek, following the dogs in pursuit of a fox. The moment they left, I hopped out of the rumble seat of the Model A Coupe and got inside the car with Mom and Shirley to wait for their return.

After a short while, I looked up and thought I saw Granddad coming toward us from the woods.

"Granddad!" I stuck my head out the window and hollered, but as the large figure grew closer, I quickly realized that it was not Granddad, but something else.

We all stared wide-eyed at a huge, hairy creature that walked upright as tall, if not taller, than a man, too far away to discern any distinct features.

"What is that?" Mom watched as it crossed in front of us and headed toward the creek.

Even from a distance, we heard it plowing through the bushes, leading us to conceptualize its immense size.

"I don't know," I told her. "But it sure looks big."

Minutes later, Daddy and Granddad returned and told us that something sizeable was moving through the woods and had trampled past them down by the creek, snapping branches as it ran away from the dogs. We told them what we'd just seen, and Daddy figured it was most likely a bear, but the mention of bigfoot did arise in conversation a few times, and even in joking, it left one to wonder.

So, getting back to that eerie night out on Hurrikin with Ronald, the thought of a mysterious creature wandering that swamp—a huge, hairy figure that walked upright like a man—spooked me.

"What animal would make those sounds?" Ronald moved fast along the bank.

"I'm not sure." I didn't mention my thoughts of bigfoot. "Just keep movin'." A cold shiver ran down my spine.

Ronald and I continued to follow the bank toward home, and the menacing sounds grew closer and louder as we went, shrieks and yawps that I then came to derive was coming from the trees. That was somewhat of a relief, as bigfoot would not be pursuing us from the trees, but that left me to ponder the question: What would?

"Wait a second." I came to a sudden stop, catching a distinct and identifiable hoot that told me what it was we were fleeing. "You're not going to believe this." I looked at Ronald and laughed. "It's owls...just a bunch of owls."

"Owls?" Ronald listened.

"It sounds like at least five." I felt a little foolish.

"Why are they makin' all of those weird noises tonight, like people hollerin'?"

"I'm not sure. I've never heard a group of so many together at one time before, much less making sounds like ancient tribal warriors calling out to one another."

Despite the relief of knowing that there was no swamp monster or bigfoot stalking us that night, I still felt unsettled, as though something wasn't quite right; so, Ronald and I headed on home. I had no explanation for the unusual behavior of the owls, chalking it up to just another adventure out on Hurrikin, with this one bein' one fowl hootenanny and quite a parliamentary stir.

* * * *

I STOOD IN THE DOORWAY of our little house, staring past our front porch and into the night, listening to Mom and Daddy talk about a small Farmall tractor Daddy had recently acquired, hardly able to hear them over the roar of rain pounding our tin roof. Lighting popped and branched across the sky in explosive chaos, and I quickly ducked back inside. It was the worst thunderstorm we'd had in months, and it showed no signs of letting up anytime soon. To make matters worse, we had been caught unprepared, having run out of lamp oil, leaving us with only the fireplace to light the house.

"Red, how 'bout you take Ronald and run over to the neighbors and borrow some oil and a couple of lamps." Daddy pointed north, indicating the neighbors he was referring to. "We'll take 'em back when I buy some oil in a day or two."

I walked toward the table where he and Mom were sitting. "It's rainin' cats and dogs outside."

"A little rain ain't gonna hurt you." Daddy gripped a mason jar half full of sweet tea.

"No one's there. They all left for Milledgeville yesterday," I reminded him.

"Just go on in. They won't mind." Daddy took a

sip from his glass.

I wasn't keen on the idea. The family had recently suffered a personal crisis, and I didn't feel comfortable about going into their home while they were away.

"Don't worry. I told them we'd keep an eye on the place while they're gone, and that could be for some time to come."

I knew arguing was pointless, so I grabbed my jacket, and along with Ronald, headed out into the storm. We made a mad dash for the branches (runs off the main creek), ducking our heads down as lighting flashed overhead. Luckily, it didn't take long to reach the neighbor's place, as it was just across the branches.

"I don't want to go in there. It's spooky." Ronald stopped and stared at house.

"No one's here." I headed for the porch to get out of the storm.

Fierce wind whipped rain onto the old porch that creaked and moaned as we hesitated at the door. My heart skipped a beat when a tree branch grated against the side of the house, creating an unnerving sound like fingernails scraping a chalkboard, sending the hair on the back of my neck standing on end.

"I really don't want to go in there." Ronald remained hesitant. "I sure wish we had a light with us. It's so dark."

"Yeah." Under the circumstances, I was a little nervous myself.

I knocked on the door just to be certain no one was home before pushing it open, knowing the house would be unlocked, as no one back then locked their doors. In Handtown, our doors were always open.

"Let's just grab what we came for and get out of here." I stepped inside, and an icy shiver swept up my spine. "They always keep a lamp in the second room."

Even though the family had only been gone a day, entering the dark house amid a raging storm, the dwelling felt cold and hollow.

"I don't like bein' in here," Ronald whispered as if fearing someone, other than the two of us, might overhear. "Red?" His voice quivered. "Red?"

"I'm right here," I assured him. "I can't find any oil, but I've got a lamp. We just need one more."

"Ahhh!" Ronald suddenly hollered.

I nearly dropped the lamp. "What's wrong?"

"It's moving!" he shrieked.

"What's moving?" I looked for him in the dark room, scarcely able to discern the outline of his body a few feet away.

"The chair...it's rockin'. Somebody's in that chair!" He scrambled for the door, making a ruckus as he bolted across the wooden floor in his haste to escape. "Somebody's in that chair!"

I walked to the door just as a bolt of lightning lit up the sky, and I caught a glimpse of Ronald hightailin' it for the branches. I don't think I'd ever seen him more scared.

"You done thought a ghost was rockin' in that chair, about to getcha."

I laughed, knowing I was the culprit responsible for the chair scare, 'cause I'd unintentionally pushed down on the arm of the old rocker as I'd moved past it in the dark room.

I laughed again and continued looking for a second lamp, finally finding some oil and one more lamp in the far corner of the front room. I quickly grabbed them up and headed out, met by Ronald on the porch.

"You came back." I was surprised.

"Who is in there?" Ronald, drippin' wet, peered through the open door from a safe distance.

"No one's in there." I told him what happened. "I thought for sure you'd run all the way home. You would have had one sensational story for Mom, Daddy, and Shirley."

"I wasn't gonna leave you."

I handed him one of the lamps. "Let's go."

We ran for the branches, lightning cracking and wind whipping as we headed for home. The dark, stormy conditions had made for quite an active night that we'd not soon forget, but in the end, we all got a good laugh out of Ronald's chair scare.

LATTER TEEN YEARS

In 1951, besides that being the year I turned 18 years old, two major events occurred that completely changed my life. First, in March of that year, my family said Goodbye to Grandma Sears who died at the age of 73 from complications that arose following a fall that had resulted in a fractured hip. After her passing, Granddad's farm never felt quite the same to me, and all of Handtown experienced a great loss, for she was much loved.

Secondly, in October of 1951, God had blessed our family with a new addition, my youngest sibling,

Glynn. That was a nerve-racking day I'll never forget 'cause Daddy was not home when Mom went into labor—he worked a part-time job as a school bus driver in those days—and I had no idea what to do.

"The baby's coming." Mom was having contractions. "Red, you're gonna have to drive me to the doctor. We'll leave a note so everyone will know what happened."

I grabbed Mom's bag and helped her out to Daddy's Model A Coupe, so nervous I could hardly think straight. I jumped behind the wheel and peeled out of the driveway in a cloud of red dust, floorin' it like a moonshine runner.

"Slow down." Mom was bouncing in her seat.

Terrified that she might give birth before I got her to a doctor in McRae (a town northwest of Hazlehurst), I kept the pedal to the metal, covering ground in record time. Reaching the northern end of Yawn Cemetery, I turned right, crossed over Hurrikin, and had just reached the next ridge when the tires caught a sandy area on the edge of the roadway and sent the car sliding out of control. Without stopping, we bounced across a shallow ditch and sideswiped a bunch of palmettos before veering back across the ditch and returning to the road.

"Are you okay, Mom?"

The mishap had bounced her around worse than a bobbin' bobber on choppy waters.

"I'm fine." She rubbed her belly and moaned. "You just need to slow down and take it easy."

Gripping the wheel, I took a deep breath, let up on the gas pedal, and continued on to McRae without further incident, finally able to breathe when we pulled up to a small clinic, and I got Mom inside. Daddy, Shirley, and Ronald later joined us at the clinic, and that night, my youngest brother, Glynn, made his debut appearance, literally arriving—thanks to my driving—a bouncing baby boy.

* * * *

I USED TO GO HUNTING now and again, but I really loved fishing, and I went every chance I got. I'd take Ronald with me fishin' down on Hurrikin, often to a spot we called Trash Lake—a branch directly behind our farm—or at the Big Lake located behind Uncle Thomas's place to our south. We'd sometimes go at night to set out hooks to catch catfish. In the springtime, rains would come and swell the creek onto the banks, and we'd set hooks all out in the shallow water and walk logs across the runs. A flooded creek made for great fishin', and I knew some perfect spots for trotlines. Ronald was just a kid, not more than ten years old, but I looked after him. He'd follow me around like a shadow, sticking close, never getting more than a few feet away as I checked the hooks for fish and strung up any we'd caught. Sometimes we'd run those hooks till ten or eleven o'clock at night before heading home.

I remember one night when my cousin Judon and our friend Dubb came along, and the four of us headed down to the creek—me, Ronald, Dubb, and Judon—to set out some lines. It was a dark and cloudy evening, and I led the way, carrying a lantern that cast a hazy circle of light as we set out hooks. An amplified buzz of cicadas surrounded us, and a breeze picked up as we meandered the creek, the wind blowing just strong enough to stir the tree limbs and underbrush. I could tell that Ronald was a bit nervous in the dark, shadowy woods, hovering so close that had I taken one step backward, I'd have stepped on him. Dubb followed Ronald, and Judon brought up the rear, trusting my lead that dark night.

We followed the mucky bank, coming to a deep area of the creek where I knew we could cross over a log that spanned the width of the waterway, but due to recent rains, I found the log lying obscured under several inches of water. I glanced back at Ronald and told him to watch his footing, and I started across the submerged log, balancing through ankle-deep water, nearly reaching the opposite side when—

KERSPLOSH!

I spun around, jolted by the sound of something heavy falling into the water, afraid it might have been Ronald. Thankfully, he was fine, and Dubb too, but I didn't see Judon. Then, to my surprise, my cousin sprung up from the water like some mythical water creature rising from the dark depths, gurgling out a yell, having stepped right off the bank and into the deep water that swallowed him whole and spit him back out.

"Are you okay?" I handed Ronald the lantern and helped Judon out of the water, pushing away one of our dogs that had followed us from the house as they often did.

"Didn't you see the log?" Dubb laughed, holding onto a string of fish.

"I'm literally walkin' blind behind the rest of ya." Judon did the wet dog shake to dry off, and the dog, wet from swimming across the creek, did the same, spraying everyone with water. "You didn't warn me that the log's underwater, and I missed my step."

Despite the incident, we continued with our fishin' excursion, me, Ronald, and Dubb in our wet boots and my cousin drippin' wet from head to toe, all of us getting a good laugh out of Judon's KERSPLOSH! misstep.

* * * *

DUBB WAS A GOOD FRIEND, and we had some fun times together, getting into a little trouble now and again, as with the infamous thermometer explosion when we were a few years younger and still in school. As we transitioned from our early teen years to our latter ones, we continued doin' a few things we ought not to be doin', but at that age and stage of development, I'd decided that what Mama didn't know wouldn't hurt her, as the saying goes.

One day, Dubb and I were driving home from Hazlehurst in his dad's car when a truck ran a stop sign and hit our vehicle flat in the side.

"Dad just got this car." Dubb was beside himself with angst over the collision.

Even though the accident wasn't our fault, Dubb knew his dad would be livid, but on the bright side, at least no one was hurt. So, we left the scene and drove on home to Dubb's house, where he tried to hide the damage to the car from his dad by parking the vehicle in front of their house in such a way that only the good side was visible. I knew he was dreading the task of facing his dad, but I also knew that his vain attempt to hide the damage wouldn't keep him out of trouble for long.

"This won't work, Dubb. He's gonna find out sooner or later."

"He might just tan my hide," Dubb fretted, "so, the later, the better."

With nothing more to be done, I left my woeful friend to face the consequences alone, and I walked home. I didn't see Dubb again till the following week, but I was relieved to find him back to his usual self, and doubly glad to hear that his hide still remained untanned.

Approaching the age of 19, I really wanted a car of my own, and Daddy told me I could earn money by raising some hogs that I could keep in the cornfield. So, when I had earned enough money to buy my first hog, Daddy took me in his Model A Coupe to see a man who sold me a thoroughbred Poland China pig for $25. I scooped up the piglet, held it in my lap while riding home, and started breeding and raising pigs.

It took some time, but eventually my Poland China pig enterprise paid off, and I used the money from the sale of those pigs to purchase my first car—a used two-door 49 Ford. I had gone to the Ford dealership in Hazlehurst to look around, learning that a local schoolteacher happened to be there trading in her car for a new one. I really liked the car she was trading in, so when the dealership offered me a good price for it, I seized the moment and bought it on the spot. The car was green, had a few thousand miles on it, and in prime condition. It was a fortunate happenstance, and I couldn't have been happier...like a Poland China pig in mud.

The following Sunday morning, I was looking forward to driving my new car to church, excited to show it off to my friends who hadn't yet seen it. Mom, Shirley, and Ronald had already left for church, and I lollygagged around the house, not minding the time, until I was running late.

"Service has already started." Daddy wasn't feeling well that morning and had decided to stay home. "You'd better get goin', son." He ushered me out the door.

I hopped in my car and headed for the church, knowing Mom would be watching for me. Upon reaching the end of Yawn Cemetery, I rolled to a stop and laughed while glancing across the road at the sight of a bible verse painted across the side of a tobacco barn, big as a billboard. There was nothing funny about the verse, mind you, but the circumstance of it being displayed in such a manner that tickled my funny bone every time I saw it.

A while back, during a Sunday school meeting, a heated debate over the topic of baptism and the scripture Luke 23:43 had arisen between one of my aunts and the owner of that barn, which had induced his actions. She must have really made him hoppin' mad to have brought about such an outcome, but he'd gotten his point across in a big way, and continued to do so, 'cause every time my aunt went to church, she had to pass by that tobacco barn, and his message was one that could not be missed.

Continuing on, I made a left turn and hurried up the road to the church. I pulled in and was circling the building to park when I unexpectedly collided head-on with another car that was rounding the church from the opposite direction.

I jumped out of my car, completely shaken. "Are you okay?"

By the sound of the impact, I knew there was damage.

"I'm fine," the man I'll refer to as Brother Bob assured me.

"I'm so sorry about this." I felt responsible.

"It's as much my fault as yours." Brother Bob assessed the damage. "Both of us runnin' late for service, and both of us rounding that corner a little too fast."

"My new car." My heart sank.

I was thankful that no one was hurt, but the impact had torn up the front end of my newly purchased 49 Ford that I'd worked so hard to save the money to buy.

"What happened?" A church member approached from the front of the building. "We heard a crash."

"Just a little fender bender," Brother Bob answered. "We're both fine."

By then, several people had gathered around both cars that sat at the back, northeast corner of the church, blocking the dirt drive between the woods and the building.

"If you'd been on time and inside the church, where you shoulda been, this wouldn't a happened," a man whom I'll call Brother Isaac sounded off, a fella known for speaking his mind.

The last thing I needed at that moment was a snide remark, but Brother Isaac was the man who'd bought my pigs I'd raised to buy my new car, so being thankful to him in that regard, I ignored his comment.

Heavy-hearted, I skipped service and drove back home, worried how Daddy would react to me wrecking the car. When I pulled up to the house, I sat outside for several minutes before trudging inside to face him.

"What are you doing back home?" Daddy instantly knew something was wrong.

I told him what had happened, expecting him to be upset with me, but he wasn't the least bit mad. I guess he figured my disappointment and state of distress over the damage to my new car was punishment enough.

"Well, that's okay," he said quite calmly. "Accidents happen."

The next day, Daddy went with me to drop my car off at a garage in Douglas, where they kept it for a few days and fixed it up good as new. The morning he drove me back to pick it up, I climbed behind the wheel of my green two-door 49 Ford, so glad to be back on the road again. I couldn't have been more thankful to Daddy for his help and understanding, and I was, without a doubt, a little wiser due to the whole experience. As the old proverb says: Experience is the best teacher.

DRAFTED

One of the biggest events to impact my life occurred in 1953, the year I'd been drafted into the Army to serve in the Armed Forces just as the fighting in Korea had ceased. The Universal Military Training and Service Act had required all males between the ages of 18 and 26 to register for the draft, and just like so many other young men across the United States at that time, I abided by the laws of our country. I had registered at the age of 18, and I was drafted at the age of 20.

Being drafted was a terrifying ordeal for a small-town farm boy. I'll never forget the day Mom brought me the dreaded letter stamped Selective Service System—the order to report for induction. Daddy and I were out in the field breakin' corn off the stalks when I spotted her running toward us from the back of the house.

"Red," she yelled, "you've been drafted!"

As she drew closer, I saw tears streaming down her face and my knees suddenly weakened at the sight of an envelope and letter gripped in her hand. My heart rate sped, and I dropped an ear of corn I was clutching, fearing the contents of that letter and how it might forever change all of our lives.

"It just came, son." With a shaky hand, she handed me the letter.

I glanced over the document, and my gaze froze on an official seal stamped at the top center of the letter, directly below five life-altering words: ORDER TO REPORT FOR INDUCTION. There was no doubt, the order to report was legitimate. I had been drafted into the armed forces—the U.S. Army.

"I don't want you to go." Mom continued to cry.

"The fighting over in Korea just stopped only a few weeks ago. I don't want you gettin' sent over there."

"Nothing's gonna happen to me, Mom." I put up a brave front to ease her fears, but in truth, I was panic-stricken about going anywhere.

I was downright petrified beyond words about being called to duty, but there was no evading the draft, and I had no other choice except to comply with my order to report for induction. The knowledge that one of my cousins had recently returned home after having served a two-year term, with one year spent in Korea, did little to lessen my anxiety. All I had ever known were the farmlands of South Georgia. I knew nothing beyond my little corner of the world, and now I was in danger of being shipped off to another country that had been actively engaged in war up to a mere eight weeks prior.

The fighting had stopped at the end of July, and upon receiving my induction letter, it was then the end of September. Still, the uncertainty, the unknown, and the prospect of dying weighed heavily on my mind. I tried not to dwell on my fears, reminding myself of my patriotic lineage—I am descended from a long line of individuals who'd served in our country's many wars dating all the way back to the Revolutionary War—and I considered the fear each of them must have experienced upon being called to duty. Those thoughts then instilled within me a sense of honor, duty, and pride for home and country that helped me come to terms with the fact that it was my turn to step up to the plate and do my part, and in doing so, that there was no shame in being afraid.

Until that moment, I don't think I'd ever fully appreciated my Christian upbringing, but upon being drafted, I got serious with God and did some major praying. I couldn't help wondering what God's future plans were for me, or if I'd even have a future destiny. I was still quite immature at the age of 20, certainly not prepared for such a huge step; but, ready or not, two weeks later, I was in a car en route to Jacksonville, scheduled to catch a bus to Fort Jackson in South Carolina. It was hard to say goodbye to Mom and Daddy, but I kept up a brave front, hugged them goodbye, and boarded that bus. I waved as it pulled away, silently crying, already missing home. For the first time in my life, I was on my own.

I entered the Army on November 3, 1953, reporting to Fort Jackson, S.C., where I was sworn in after being subjected to a physical that determined me to be physically and mentally fit for service. A few days later, I found myself boarding a bus full of other troops bound for Camp Gordon near Augusta, where I went through a processing procedure with additional testing, got immunizations (seven shots at one time), was shorn with my induction haircut, and was issued a uniform. By that time, I looked like a soldier, but I still felt like a farm boy.

This was the start of boot camp, and I was assigned to a squad for eight weeks of basic training. The last thing I wanted was trouble, so I kept my mouth shut and did what I was told, doing all I could to avoid the wrath of the drill sergeants who did a lot of shouting and making life miserable for a select few.

Days were routine, starting off early each morning with physical training before breakfast, then skilled training, lunch, and more training. We were assigned an M16A4 rifle. We learned, among other things, bayonet combat, hand to hand combat, how to march, how to scale a wall, how to dig a foxhole, and how to fire a machine gun and grenade launcher. During some of the obstacle courses, I'd skinned my knees and elbows raw. It was all very challenging, but having been a hunter and outdoorsman since boyhood, I fared better than others. All in all, I'd kept my nose clean and paid attention, knowing my purpose for being there was to serve and defend my country.

It wasn't until I'd completed boot camp that I started seeing myself as a soldier, and with the accomplishment of basic training behind me, I was granted a short leave and went back home for two weeks. It was great to see the family and that little house again, and I made the most of my time home. I went hunting, fishing, and palled around with my friends, which, on occasion, led to trouble.

One such night, I had gone out with some of my cousins and a friend of ours, whose names I will not mention, wanting to get in several last hurrahs before I shipped out. My friend's dad had just bought a brand-new car that he'd entrusted to us for the evening, and we were all hyped up and out to have a good time. Driving home from a movie, we were messing around, looking for something more to do, and we just happened to have had some cherry bomb firecrackers in our possession.

"I bet these would blow a mailbox sky high," one of the guys said. "We should try it."

That's all it took to lead us to make a really bad choice by deciding to act on what he'd suggested—to blow up a mailbox. So, we took out those cherry bombs, wound three together by their fuses, and eased up to a mailbox where we didn't think we'd be seen. We lit them, threw them inside, shut the lid, and sped away. Looking back, I watched as that mailbox rocketed a good 15 feet into the air, burst apart as its top blew off, and the mangled remains crash back down to the ground.

"Wow! Did you see how high that sucker went?" one of my cousins said. "We've gotta do that again."

Laughing and carrying-on, we continued to cherry bomb more mailboxes, including one belonging to a family member. Our actions were immature and irresponsible, and we'd gone too far with our overwrought behavior, never considering the magnitude of the vandalism we were carrying out. We knew folks would be mad to find their mailboxes blown up, especially my uncle, but we didn't realize that we were committing a federal crime—a felony. We didn't consider the aftereffect of our actions; the possibility of facing future consequences did not even occur to us at that time. Our only thought was the thrill of the moment...what might be our last hurrah!

Nearing home, we thought we'd gotten away with our mischief scot-free, until one of the fellas made a fumble and dropped the next bundle of lit cherry bombs in the back seat, sending three of us in harm's way scrambling into the front seat to escape the explosion. Amid the chaos, my friend, who was driving, slammed on the brakes and the car skidded to a stop along the shoulder of the road, but it was too late to prevent the inevitable.

BAM!

Those three cherry bombs exploded and burnt a plate-sized hole smack-dab in the middle of the back seat of that shiny, new car.

"No, no, no." My friend jumped out of the car. "How bad is it?" He yanked open the back door to assess the damage.

With ears ringing from the blast, the rest of us fell over each other as we poured out of the smoke-filled vehicle, coughing, and making sure no one was hurt.

"I can't believe this." My friend paced back and forth with arms flailing, having a meltdown. "Dad's new car. He's gonna kill me." He looked in the back seat again as the smoke cleared. "What am I gonna tell him? I can't tell him we were blowin' up mailboxes."

My cousins and I rattled off a few suggestions, none of which were too believable.

"This is a disaster. I'm dead. DEAD!" My friend raved.

On that unfortunate note, our wild night came to an end, and we all parted ways and headed home. Climbing into bed that night, I felt bad for my friend, wondering what he'd tell his dad about the damaged seat. Weighed down by guilt and regret, I tossed and turned most of the night, wishing I could go back in time and change what we'd done.

I woke the next morning, waiting all day for the other shoe to drop, but word of the cherry bomb incident never reached Mom and Daddy. So, after enjoying several more days at home, with my leave at its end, I returned to Camp Gordon thinking we were in the clear. I never would have expected the continued fallout that followed, later told by Daddy that postal inspectors had come 'round the farm making inquiries and looking to question us boys on a matter of mailbox vandalism. One of my cousins who'd been involved that night happened to be tapping trees for turpentine with Daddy the day those inspectors came by our house, and they put him through the wringer.

"I d-d-don't know...I—" Under pressure of interrogation, he stumbled over his words. I d-don't know what you're talkin' about." He denied any knowledge.

According to Daddy, the postal inspectors then asked for me by name, but he informed them that I was back at Camp Gordon. They went on to say that they were going to contact me at the base to question me about the mailbox vandalism, but fortunately, I never heard anything from them.

I, along with the rest of my cherry bomb squad, remained worried about those postal inspectors for some time to come, not sure if they might return for further inquiries. Thankfully, they never did. We also wondered who had turned us in for the vandalism, catchin' some back-fence talk that my uncle had caught sight of us that night and blew the whistle. I couldn't believe that a family member had ratted us out, but then again, we did blow his mailbox sky high, so to be fair, we had it comin'. It's as I've often heard said: Family loyalty only goes so far.

The cherry bomb incident was a lesson learned, and a memory that still lingers strongly in my mind to present day. I've never forgotten our critical lack of judgment that night and how lucky we were to have escaped what could have been severe consequences of our actions. I've never forgotten the guilt over wronging my uncle. I've never forgotten my friend and the hole we blew in the back seat of his dad's new car. I've never forgotten the thrill of those mailboxes rocketing sky high. It was our last hurrah, a story I probably shouldn't be sharing, considering the crime; however, with the statute of limitations on our act of vandalism long expired and most of us boys now in our lattermost decades of life or deceased, I reckon there is no crime in telling what we had done all those years ago. We really were just good ol' boys; we just didn't always make the best choices.

IN THE ARMY NOW

In February of 1954, while stationed at Camp Gordon, I was going through an 8-week course at the QM School for special training in laundry & dry cleaning when Daddy and Uncle Thomas traveled to the base to request my discharge from service due to family hardship. Daddy had been sick and needed me home to work the farm, so in an effort to make that happen, he'd obtained letters of treatment and disability from his doctors in Hazlehurst stating that he was unable to work due to his condition, hoping that the documentation would be enough for the military to grant me a complete discharge and separation from active duty.

Sitting in an office with Daddy and Uncle Thomas, I was somewhat intimidated by a colonel who was reviewing my case. He leaned back in a big chair and studied the medical documents Daddy had presented him, not saying much, other than an occasional hmm, as he listened to the many reasons why I was needed back at home.

"Hey, Private Sears." That ol' colonel suddenly straightened in his chair, put the papers down, and looked directly at me. "So, you want to get out, huh?"

I said, "Well, sir, I guess so. They're trying to get me out 'cause I'm needed at home. So, I guess I should."

"Well, guess what?" He opened a drawer and pulled out a form. "You're headed to Fort Lee, Virginia, to the WAC (Women's Army Corps) area. There are plenty of girls there."

I think my mouth fell somewhat agape, and I didn't know what to say.

"Do you like girls?" he asked me.

"Yes sir," I answered. "As good as any other fella."

I knew Daddy wasn't happy with the direction our meeting had taken, but it was obvious that the colonel had not been convinced that a hardship discharge was in order.

"Private Sears," the colonel stood up, "that's where you're going, to Fort Lee to guard the WAC."

Needless to say, I was not granted a hardship discharge that day, and Daddy and Uncle Thomas left for home without success. After that meeting, I wasn't sure if I'd actually get sent to guard the WAC, but soon, just as the colonel had stated, I received orders for transfer to Fort Lee, Virginia, where I was placed on nighttime guard duty. I remember walking the blocks, seeing a lot of things out of some of those girls that I blush to remember, but it was quite a developmental experience, which I presume was precisely what that ol' colonel had intended.

I wasn't at Fort Lee long before learning that I would soon be heading to South Korea, and four weeks later, in April of 1954, I was sitting on a bus full of troops, preparing to leave for a country where a war had not long ended. Over eight months had passed since the fighting had ceased, and Operation Glory was happening at that time, with casualties of the war continuing to be returned home—the many brave soldiers who had lost their lives over in Korea. The fighting had stopped, but in the aftermath, people remained wary.

Sitting on that bus, the driver was just about to pull out when an officer stepped aboard and called out my name, along with three others, informing us that our orders had been changed. So, we got off the bus, soon learning that we were being deployed to Germany instead of South Korea. Even though the fighting had ended the previous July, I was glad for the change of orders, and soon found myself boarding another bus, this time leaving Fort Lee bound for the Brooklyn Army Base located on Brooklyn's western shore in New York, where I would stay for a few days before embarking on a troopship for Germany.

The Brooklyn Army Base was a massive military post and terminal consisting of double-decked piers, docks, multi-level warehouses, and a large rail yard with five tracks, two of which ran through one of the large warehouses. I had been told that there was also a military prison located there, which I never saw, but the enormity of the base was intimidating, far exceeding anything I had imagined. It was a big, big, big world out there, and I was far from home, and soon to go even farther.

Leaving the Brooklyn Army Base, an Army band played as I boarded a U.S. Navy transport ship that was at least 600 feet in length and towered to a height of what must have been a hundred feet to the top of her double funnels (smokestacks). I stood on deck, staring at the Statue of Liberty raising her torch over Upper New York Bay as we pulled away from the pier. I marveled at the surrounding cityscape beyond Governors Island, high-rise buildings towering in Jersey City and Lower Manhattan Island, separated by the Hudson River. We then moved through the Narrows, past the New York Harbor on Staten Island, heading into the Lower Bay that opened into the North Atlantic. I swallowed hard and my stomach knotted, but at this point, there was no turning back. I was about to cross the mighty ocean.

The first couple of days aboard the ship weren't too bad; I suffered from unpleasant bouts of seasickness, but not so intolerable that I couldn't cope. However, on our fourth or fifth day out at sea, we ran into a severe storm, with waves so high that I feared the ship might capsize. The soldiers, all seasick from the rough seas, stayed up on deck as long as the crew permitted, heaving over the side of the vessel. In that moment, I didn't think things could get any worse, but as the storm further intensified, we were ordered inside the transport, where crew members and passengers were throwing up all over every square inch of that ship. There was no escaping the profusion of vomit. It was the beatinest mess I'd ever seen. Everyone was heaving, and I threw up with the rest of 'em, my stomach turning somersaults as the bow of that big ol' troopship repeatedly rose and fell with those high waves, the vessel battered by that fierce storm that rolled her so far over onto her side that it terrified me. I'd never been so sick, or scared, wondering if I might die—meet my watery end out there in the middle of the North Atlantic.

Nauseous and in a sweat, I returned to my sleeping quarters, a crowded compartment containing rows of stacked bunks that left very little wiggle room for the lower-level occupants. Lying down, I tried to ignore the foul stench of vomit that filled my nostrils, pitifully moaning as the ship rocked and rolled on those turbulent seas. I never thought the storm would pass, but after a while, the winds calmed, and the seas finally died down.

I rolled out of my bunk and headed topside to see if I could go on deck and get some desperately needed fresh air. I had expected to find improved conditions aboard the ship, but to my dismay, everyone was still sick and throwing up. I tried to block out the smell and forge onward through the stink and mess all around me, but my gag reflex joined the chain reaction, and I started heaving. To make matters worse, at that moment, the ol' captain of that ship happened to come walking by and stopped to address me.

"Soldier." He asked my name and rank.

"Private Sears," he then said, "find yourself a mop and bucket and start cleaning this mess up."

I stood there, trying not to upchuck, thinking: Lord have mercy. I said it once, and I'll say it again: That was the beatinest mess I'd ever seen. It was, to put it mildly, nasty, but between the crew and troops, we eventually got that ship cleaned up.

That was one foul experience that left me with the smell of vomit in my nostrils for days, but it didn't halt our voyage; we were 14 days on the water, and I stayed nauseous the entire time. I remember feeling enormous relief when we finally reached Bremerhaven, Germany, so much so that I could have kissed the ground of that foreign land, 'cause after that harsh voyage, any land was preferable to sea.

Marching off that ship at the port of Bremerhaven—a long, spread-out port at the mouth of the river Weser that opened into the North Sea—I stood in formation, marveling at the thought of entering the Gateway to Europe—the Old World. I would have liked to have seen more of Bremerhaven, but my journey continued the following day, when I boarded a train to travel to Mannheim, Germany. Along our route, the train made occasional stops as it passed through stations, where local children would rush the train, running alongside, begging for handouts. Soldiers would toss them the likes of candy bars, apples, sometimes money, whatever they could spare.

It took a day to make it over to Mannheim, then from there, I was sent on to my assigned location—the 15th Quartermaster Battalion in Seckenheim, Germany. The headquarters consisted of the 22nd Quartermaster Subsistence Supply Company, the 520th Quartermaster Company (petroleum supply), and the 526th Quartermaster Company (petroleum supply). At that time, I was a member of the Quartermaster Corps (QMC) for laundry & dry cleaning, but upon my very first day there, my superior decided to transfer me from laundry & dry-cleaning duty to special police duty, to work as a guard at the QM Headquarters. So, from that day forth, my new job was to guard the gates, with 526th QM Company my most significant duty assignment.

I considered myself lucky to be a guard at the QM Headquarters, 'cause the captain that was over me and six other guards never gave any inspections or let anyone mess with us. We had a lot of leisure time, set our own work habits, and things ran relatively smoothly for 1 year, 6 months, and 5 days.

I had two main duties while stationed in Germany, one was guarding the main gate, and the other was flag detail. The latter was a job I was proud to perform, despite some of those mornings being dreadfully cold. Three guards would go out twice daily to raise and lower the American flag as a bugle call played over a loudspeaker. In the morning ceremony, the flag was raised at 6:30 a.m. to the short tune

"Reveille" to indicate the start of the day's activities. Then, we'd return at 5 p.m. to the sound of another bugle call "Retreat", and we'd lower the flag as "To the Colors" played, marking the end of the day's activities. Soldiers' lives were regulated by bugle calls, keeping our days routine, with the melody "Taps" being the final call of the day, signaling lights out and the start of quiet hours.

I was also sent out on maneuvers a few times, with one particular incident occurring that I'll never forget. One bitterly cold and icy night, while out in the boondocks on a winter maneuver, my company had stopped to hunker down till morning. We parked the trucks and started digging snow trenches, with some of the men staking pup tents over the trenches they'd dug for additional protection from the cold.

"I guess we'd better start digging." I stood with one of my buddies, looking for a good spot to hunker down, suddenly getting a bright idea, as I was prone to do. "What about there?" I motioned toward the six or more military trucks parked a short distance away. "The best place, as far as I can see, is under one of those."

In agreement, my comrade and I slipped over to a supply truck and crawled under the front of it, dug out an area, settled in with blankets, and fell asleep. Sometime later, in the mid of night, we were suddenly startled awake by the vrooming engine of that truck cranking up.

"I guess we're movin' out." I told the other fella, but before we were able to crawl out from under the truck, it suddenly pulled forward, forcing us to duck low to clear the undercarriage.

"Woah." My heart rate sped to a gallop as the vehicle's big wheels rolled past me on each side. "They're leavin' us." I scrambled to my feet, grabbed my blankets, and along with my comrade, swung myself into the back of that supply truck as it pulled away, the two of us scarcely making it by the skin of our teeth.

Unbeknownst to us, the company had been awakened and told that it was time to move out. The other men had loaded up in the transport trucks, but being asleep under the supply truck, my buddy and I hadn't heard the order to load up, and we nearly got left out there in the frozen boondocks.

"I bet we're gonna be in hot water for this," my cohort moaned.

I figured he was right, but I was too tired to dwell on our troubles and settled down for the long ride back to base. It was bitter cold in the back of that truck, so I covered up under my blankets and nodded off, later waking when we'd reached the base. As soon as the truck parked, we scrambled out of the back, fully expected some course of reprimand for our escapade. We saw that our company was unloading from the transport trucks and covertly maneuvered in their direction, deciding to ease back in with them on the q.t. To our relief, no one seemed to notice our surreptitious infiltration, or that we had been absent up to that point. So, with none the wiser, we acted as though we'd been there all along...just dumb luck.

By that time, I had been stationed in Seckenheim, Germany for nearly a year, still performing my duties as a guard, which sometimes included guarding prisoners. I remember one particular prisoner whom I'd been assigned to escort to the mess hall for meals, and during our time together, we'd talk.

One day, he'd asked me, "If I were to run for that fence and try to escape, what would you do?"

I told him, "I don't know what I'd do. I can say, if you run, we're gonna catch you."

Luckily, he never put me in a position to be forced to respond to any such action, but that question he'd asked me that day always lingered in my mind, leaving me to wonder: If he'd ran, what would I have done?

I usually had plenty to write home about, and I wrote often in response to Mom's letters and care packages that were always a blessing to receive. She kept me up to date on the day-to-day happenings back home—the good and the bad. I was sorry to learn that the crop season that year had been a poor one, forcing Daddy to buy more necessities on credit than usual, which led to mounting debt. There wasn't a lot that I could do to help keep the farm afloat other than to send money, so I sent all I could, withholding just enough funds to get by, with a small allowance for off-duty activities. Life on base could sometimes be dull, and when my bunkmates and I were off duty, we'd often listen to records or go to picture shows. I also did a little sightseeing outside of the base, including one memorable trip to Heidelberg Castle. Bunking with six other fellas, we'd gotten to know each other well, but after separating from the Army, we lost touch. I often wonder what became of those fellas—my Army buddies who'd made my 18-month tour of duty bearable, even fun at times. I was a long way from home, but I was in good company.

IN THE ARMY NOW

After 1 year, 6 months, and 5 days in Germany, I had fulfilled my two-year requirement of active-duty service, and it was time to head back home to the United States and separate from the Armed Forces. So, in October of 1955, I boarded a transatlantic ocean liner that was notably larger than the troopship I'd previously embarked upon, and crossed back across the North Atlantic, thankful for an uneventful second voyage—no profusion of vomit on my return trip. We, however, arrived off the shore of New York two days ahead of schedule, and the captain anchored the ship in the bay, within visual distance of the Statue of Liberty, to wait out that time. I'll never forget being up on the main deck and seeing that captain walk past me and a bunch of other soldiers, making his way to the back of the ship with a tiny fishin' rod gripped in his hand. There, he laid out a cot, tossed a line in the water, covered up with a blanket, and fell asleep. The soldiers were in a huff, antsy to get to shore, with a few individuals spouting verbal threats to jump ship and swim to the piers. There was a great deal of fuming, but we all knew that we had no choice other than to patiently wait for the ship to eventually dock, which indeed happened at its scheduled time, two days later.

Marveling one last time at the surrounding cityscape, I disembarked the ship to the cheerful welcome of an Army band. I was glad to be back in my own country, but New York was still a long way from home. I wasn't at the Brooklyn Army Base long, though, before boarding a bus bound for Fort Jackson, South Carolina, where I was honorably discharged, formally ending my active-duty military career, two years that had not only forced me to grow up, but an experience that had completely changed my outlook on life.

Still having six years of reserve time left to fulfill, I was placed on standby (I was later discharged from the Army Reserve in October of 1961), and I returned home to get back to civilian life. I was glad to be out of the military, but I wasn't thrilled about returning to crop farming. After being out in the world, I really didn't want to go back to working those red clay fields day in and day out, from sunup till sundown. I loved the farm, but I aspired to do more. So, I sat down and had a heart-to-heart conversation with Daddy about my aspirations of seeing what else I could achieve outside of working the farm, and he understood my ambitions.

Eager to prove myself, I ultimately left for Jacksonville, Florida, where I stayed with my uncle while I sought work. Having no success there, I went back to Handtown full of disappointment, but before long, I had learned of opportunities to be found in Southwest Florida. So, ready to venture further south, Daddy, being in debt at that time, decided to sell the farm, pay off his creditors, and make the bold move with me. It was a risky gamble, but we placed our lives in God's hands, trusting that He would supply all our needs.

I had no idea what future destiny God had in store for me, but at the age of 22, it was time to turn the page and start a new chapter. So, along with the whole family, I left South Georgia in search of a better future. I knew I would desperately miss the farm, as would Daddy, Mom, Shirley, Ronald, and Glynn, but no matter how far I ever roamed, I knew I would always carry my fond memories of life growing up in Handtown with me—a boy dressed in ragged overalls, heading down to the Big Lake to do some fishin'—a part of me that would forever dwell in those red hills of home.

EPILOGUE

October 2020
Handtown Community, Hazlehurst, Ga

Sitting on the edge of the old well curb that remains on land that was once my childhood homestead, I stood up and gazed in the direction of the Big Lake, wiping my teary eyes as I waved to a ghostly image in the near distance, watching as the red-headed boy from my youth slowly faded from sight.

"Wait." I called out, longing to follow him down

to Hurrikin, but upon taking a step in his direction, a familiar voice caught my ear, and I turned back.

"Hey, Grandpa. We're back." One of my grandchildren ran toward me from across Yawn Cemetery. "We saw the old tobacco barn and walked a long way through the pines."

I then saw the rest of my family come into view, and my heart lifted. I had a lot to be thankful for.

"Sorry it took so long." Ronald walked over and stood next to me.

"No. I enjoyed the time by myself to revisit the past."

Ronald stared toward the Big Lake. "We had some good times out there on that creek when we were boys, didn't we?"

My eyes teared up again. "We sure did."

Ronald patted my shoulder. "God's been good to us over the years."

"He sure has." I looked at my wife standing with my three daughters, and I smiled.

God had blessed my life in so many ways, providing what I needed when I needed it, even calling

EPILOGUE

me into the ministry. Now, at the age of 87, I have been retired for many years from working as a road and bridge superintendent for Lee County in Florida, but over the years I also pastored a church, doing God's work.

"Guess we better go. Everyone's loading up." Ronald motioned. "It was a good reunion this year. Guess we'll be back to do it all again next October, God willin'."

I would be counting the days, always looking forward to seeing my old stomping grounds again, and maybe even catching another glimpse of that carefree, red-headed boy that still resides within me. For, I will always be Georgia Boy Red, and Handtown will forever remain...the red hills of home.

The
Red Hills
of Home

www.ingramcontent.com/pod-product-compliance
Lightning Source LLC
Chambersburg PA
CBHW030151100526
44592CB00009B/217